IMPROVING OUR SCHOOLS

THIRTY-THREE STUDIES THAT INFORM LOCAL ACTION

IMPROVING OUR SCHOOLS

THIRTY-THREE STUDIES THAT INFORM LOCAL ACTION

MARILYN CLAYTON FELT / EDUCATION DEVELOPMENT CENTER

With a foreword by Harold Howe II

The research and writing of this book were supported by the Ford Foundation and Education Development Center.

Education Development Center, Inc.
55 Chapel Street
Newton, Massachusetts 02160

Acknowledgments

EDUCATION DEVELOPMENT CENTER STAFF PARTICIPANTS:

Janet Whitla, President

Cheryl J. Vince, Vice President
and Director of School and Society Programs

Marc Posner, Senior Researcher
and Permissions Editor

Barbara B. Herzstein, Project Editor

Ellen Knight, Word Processing Specialist

Suzi Wojdyslawski, Designer

Thanks to the authors and researchers who gave time to review our summaries, and to Edward J. Meade, Jr., of the Ford Foundation, who believes so strongly in schools, their staffs, and their students.

Selections from **A Place Called School** by John I. Goodlad, Copyright © 1984 by the Institute for the Development of Educational Activities, Inc. Paperback Edition $9.95. Used with permission of the McGraw-Hill Book Company.

Selections from **On Further Examination,** copyright © 1977 by the College Entrance Examination Board, New York. Reprinted by permission.

Selections from **High School** by Ernest L. Boyer, copyright © 1983 by the Carnegie Foundation for the Advancement of Teaching and Harper & Row, Publishers Inc.

Selections from **Policy Options For Quality Education,** copyright © 1984 by the National Association of State Boards of Education. Reprinted by permission.

Selections from **The Paideia Proposal** by Mortimer J. Adler, copyright © 1982 by the Institute for Philosophical Research and **Paideia Problems and Possibilities** by Mortimer J. Adler, copyright © 1983 by the Institute for Philosophical Research. Reprinted with permission of Macmillan Publishing Company.

CONTENTS

FOREWORD

Twenty-five years from now educational historians will be
looking back at the early 1980s with the same time perspective that we now look at the late 1950s. One of the
questions they will then try to answer is whether the
changes in schools that grew from the discontents of
university professors and from the Sputnik-related forces
that helped to pass the National Defense Education Act of
1958 were more or less significant than the changes now
being mounted in schools as the result of the reports and
studies appearing in the early 1980s.

My guess is that those future historians will see the
present period as a more important moment of change in
the history of American schooling. I say this with no
intent to denigrate what was done for improving the
quality of American schools in the post-Sputnik era. The
modernization of the curriculum in secondary-school
science was a major contribution of the period. So was
upgrading the knowledge of many science teachers through
summer institutes sponsored by the National Science Foundation. Over the years these teachers have quietly gone
about their business for the benefit of thousands of
students. They helped to make possible one of the significant improvements in the quality of American secondary
schools.

The main reason that the current potential for changing
and improving schools seems to me to outweigh that of the
post-Sputnik period lies in the depth and complexity of
the research and recommendations available in the new
studies and reports. They reach to federal, state, and
local roles in educational change and beyond them to the
individual school and the individual classroom. They
cover almost every conceivable aspect of school activity.
If they have any major omission, it lies primarily in
their neglect of what one writer has called "the continuing equity agenda"--a concern for the educational fortunes of the poor, minorities, and other children with
special needs. But these interests were equally neglected in the reforms that originated in the 1950s. The real
question that arises from the richness of analysis and
recommendation we have before us today is whether educa-

tion's leaders can muster the skill and wisdom to put together a multiple-level set of initiatives that will gain support.

Another factor that is present in the current enthusiasm for improving school quality, the interest and support of the business community, was not nearly as evident in the earlier period. It is impossible to assess what this business interest in schooling will ultimately amount to, but there is enough going on under its banner to signal large possibilities. An $800 million school improvement legislation was passed in California with an organized push from business; most major business groups in the country are active on behalf of schools; and the Committee on Economic Development is investing substantial funds in yet another study of American schools. There were few such developments in the post-Sputnik era. Whether the interest of corporate leadership will extend to paying new state and local taxes to upgrade schools remains to be seen.

The motivation that provided the energy for the school quality improvements of the post-Sputnik period was less pervasive than that which is operating today. In the earlier period it came from two sources: the concern of college professors that the curriculum of schools was out of date, and the national resentments (and perhaps fears) when the Soviets placed a satellite in orbit before we did. The latter event had little to do with schools but was easily translated into emotional support for the National Defense Education Act, bringing the national government into the affairs of the schools in a new way.

Nowadays a more powerful connection has been forged to argue for improving school quality: the significance of education for our capacity to compete economically with the rest of the world. This economic argument about the need for well-trained and well-motivated workers is being applied internally by numerous states, which are busy seeking ways to upgrade education so that their schools can outperform their neighboring states or regions and attract new employees in high-technology businesses. The economic argument for improving school quality seems to me more pervasive than the defense-based motivations of the earlier period. There was a tone of chauvinism about the feelings aroused by Sputnik that some Americans found unappealing, but more of us seem to find a genuine element of self-interest in the connection between schools and economic prosperity. At the same time, there are those, myself among them, who think that there are real dangers in turning our thinking about the purposes of schools too far in the direction this new interest is carrying them.

If these views about the significance of today's efforts to improve schools have any validity, we educators are living at an opportune time. In this pendulum swing of positive national interest toward schools, we have the chance for a few years (no one knows how many) to turn a significant portion of the nation's energies into school improvement activities. In addition we have a resource to assist with that task: the comprehensive examination of the strengths and weaknesses of American schools provided by the numerous reports and studies that appeared in 1983-84. The outpouring of these documents within a short period of time is, in my view, unprecedented in our educational experience in this country for its volume, its diversity, and its effect on people outside the education realm.

The numerous reports, studies, and scholarly books about American schools that have emerged over the past three years have managed to catch the interest of national, state, and local political leaders, as well as that of business leaders, presidents of colleges and universities, and self-appointed saviors of the republic of every stripe. These numerous documents have appeared together in a short time, partly by coincidence, but also as the result of a special set of circumstances.

The 1970s was a period of troubled self-doubt in American life. The frustrations awakened by the Vietnam War, the decline of the civil rights movement, and the foibles of President Nixon left us doubting ourselves and our institutions, including the schools. Old political alliances that had supported education at the state and local levels fell apart, and there were significant moves to curtail educational spending in a number of states and many localities. Progress in including a larger proportion of our youth in secondary schools was lost in concerns about

declining test scores and the troubles of school desegregation, which moved north in the 1970s. These and other
forces led to a more negative public attitude toward
education generally and toward schools in particular.

I think that these developments lie behind the launching
during the late 1970s or early 1980s of some of the
studies that now fill the desks of educators. In effect,
when people think things are not going well, responsible
individuals try to find out why and what to do about it.
I suspect, for example, that this line of reasoning is
what led to the study called <u>High School</u> by Dr. Ernest L.
Boyer and the Carnegie Foundation for the Advancement of
Teaching. Secretary T. H. Bell's appointment of the
National Commission on Excellence in Education was certainly brought on by the pervasive perception that the
quality of American schools was declining.

The challenge to educators in these circumstances is to
find their way to constructive remedies through the
morass of diagnoses and prescriptions they have before
them. The many recommendations from many sources overlap
and conflict in kaleidoscopic patterns that are difficult
to follow. Some of the documents involved are political
tracts, others are fundamental studies based on laborious
years of observation in classrooms. There is no easy way
to deal with all this material. Any individual who tries
to read all the recent reports and studies must resign
from regular duties. The result of this dilemma has been
the preparation in recent months of a number of useful
summaries. Up to now these have tended to be rather
brief outlines delineating the main recommendations of
the major documents.

This book is a more comprehensive approach to dealing
with the need for a summary document. It is not an
attempt to tell educators and policy makers what to think
and/or what to do; it is instead an effort to illuminate
and clarify the agenda that has appeared from the numerous recent studies. It is an agenda that contains some
contradictions and disagreements. The final chapters
identify a core of agreement and make suggestions for
local educators who wish to start to develop their own
improvement plans.

This is, then, a book primarily for those who operate schools: for school boards, superintendents, principals, teachers, and interested parents. But it is also a book for those concerned with initiatives for schools at the state and national levels. As actions are taken in those realms, a most important consideration is that of leaving room for action at the level of the school district and the individual school. The people close to the schools will ultimately determine whether American education turns this new wave of interest into a significant forward movement.

Harold Howe II
Senior Lecturer, Harvard Graduate School of Education
Former U.S. Commissioner of Education

PREFACE

In 1981, Education Development Center published a booklet
describing 18 major research projects that were studying
American high school education and how to strengthen it.
Now, three years later, this book reports on the conclusions of many of those efforts as well as others that
were underway during that time.

Our 1981 booklet began by saying, "This is a challenging
time for schools." The challenge has not abated over the
three years, and this fact in itself is cause for encouragement, given the short life of many education causes.
Rather, public interest remains high, and throughout the
country commissions and task forces have been set up to
aid in implementation of the studies' recommendations.
Pioneering educators at all levels have started to plan
for and introduce some of the recommended changes.

The amount of reading material resulting from the studies
is voluminous: over 6,000 pages. Therefore, with Ford
Foundation support, EDC has produced this book to make
the thinking and the conclusions of the studies conven-
iently accessible to those who are responsible for education at the local level.

From almost 50 studies, we have selected 33 that contain
substantial information and advice for local action. In
chapter one we present excerpts from the studies that
convey the tone and the subject of current concerns about
the outcomes of American education. Chapter two discusses what the different studies see as the causes of
our educational problems. Chapter three summarizes findings or recommendations of each study; each summary has
been reviewed by the study author or a representative of
the study group for accuracy of reporting. Chapter four
compares the recommendations of the full range of studies
and identifies areas of agreement. Chapter five offers
information and questions designed to help local educators find a starting point for their own improvement efforts.

Education Development Center is a nonprofit organization
dedicated to human development through education. Last

year marked our twenty-fifth year of research, program development, and evaluation. Over the years we have helped to meet the educational needs of the nation by acting as a bridge between researchers and practitioners. We hope that this overview of the current research will be useful to you as you work to address the needs of students in your community.

M.C.F.

CHAPTER ONE
The Nature of the Problems

> We need to adjust our expectation for education
> reform. Part of the difficulty is the way we
> think of success--in terms of achieving our goals
> and solving problems. Rather we need to think in
> terms of making progress toward goals, and recog-
> nize that few societal problems are dealt with
> without creating important new problems. The
> measure of success, then, is not whether we have
> solved our school problems, but whether today's
> problems are "better" than yesterday's.
>
> > -- Jerome T. Murphy, Professor of Education
> > and Associate Dean, Harvard Graduate
> > School of Education

It was clear in the early 1980s that the American public
was becoming increasingly worried about the quality of
our education, especially high school education. Educators, government agencies, the business community, and
citizen groups launched research projects, commissions,
and task forces to study schooling and to consider how to
improve it. The following statements, drawn from a few
of the studies, are presented in length to indicate both
the nature of the problems that people were seeing in
American education and the intensity of their concern.

> Public education today faces...a crisis in confidence
> in which people have lost faith in the public school's
> ability to educate its students; a crisis in perfor-
> mance in which students from public schools are gradu-
> ating without basic or marketable skills necessary to
> pursue further education or a job; and a crisis in the
> concept of democracy in which officials are willing to
> writeoff a sizeable portion of the student population
> as being uneducable and unentitled to educational
> opportunities.
> > Ruth B. Love, Superintendent of the Chicago
> > Public Schools, Proceedings of the Second
> > Conference of the University/Urban Schools
> > National Task Force

The nation's public schools are in trouble. By almost every measure--the commitment and competency of teachers, student test scores, truancy and dropout rates, crimes of violence--the performance of our schools falls far short of expectation.

> Making the Grade, report of The Twentieth Century Fund Task Force on Federal Elementary and Secondary Education Policy

Our Nation is at risk. Our once unchallenged pre-eminence in commerce, industry, science, and technological innovation is being overtaken by competitors throughout the world....[Education is] only one of the many causes and dimensions of the problem, but it is the one that undergirds American prosperity, security, and civility. We report to the American people that while we can take justifiable pride in what our schools and colleges have historically accomplished and contributed to the United States and the well-being of its people, the educational foundations of our society are presently being eroded by a rising tide of mediocrity that threatens our very future as a Nation and a people. What was unimaginable a generation ago has begun to occur--others are matching and surpassing our educational attainments.

If an unfriendly foreign power had attempted to impose on America the mediocre educational performance that exists today, we might well have viewed it as an act of war. As it stands, we have allowed this to happen to ourselves. We have even squandered the gains in student achievement made in the wake of the Sputnik challenge. Moreover, we have dismantled essential support systems which helped make those gains possible. We have, in effect, been committing an act of unthinking, unilateral educational disarmament.

> A Nation at Risk, report of the National Commission on Excellence in Education

Each generation of Americans has outstripped its parents in education, in literacy, and in economic attainment. For the first time in the history of our country, the educational skills of one generation will

2

not surpass, will not equal, will not even approach, those of their parents.

Paul Copperman, as quoted in <u>A Nation at Risk</u>

The Nation that dramatically and boldly led the world into the age of technology is failing to provide its own children with the intellectual tools needed for the 21st century.

The world is changing fast. Technological know-how is spreading throughout the world--along with the knowledge that such skills and sophistication are the basic capital of tomorrow's society.

Already the quality of our manufactured products, the viability of our trade, our leadership in research and development, and our standards of living are strongly challenged. Our children could be stragglers in a world of technology. We must not let this happen: America must not become an industrial dinosaur. We must not provide our children a 1960s education for a 21st century world.

<u>Educating Americans for the 21st Century</u>, report of the National Science Board Commission on Precollege Education in Mathematics, Science and Technology

Quality of life is directly tied to our ability to think clearly amid the noise of modern life, to sift through all that competes for our attention until we find what we value, what will make our lives worth living. What we value is seldom on the surface and, when it is found, can seldom be defended from the incursions of the trivial without sustained efforts to understand it more deeply....A society in which the habits of disciplined reading, analysis, interpretation, and discourse are not sufficiently cultivated has much to fear.

National Assessment of Educational Progress

One study gave some perspective to the situation:

It is important, of course, to recognize that <u>the average citizen</u> today is better educated and more

3

knowledgeable than the average citizen of a generation ago—more literate, and exposed to more mathematics, literature, and science. The positive impact of this fact on the well-being of our country and the lives of our people cannot be overstated. Nevertheless, the average graduate of our schools and colleges today is not as well-educated as the average graduate of 25 or 35 years ago, when a much smaller proportion of our population completed high school and college. The negative impact of this fact likewise cannot be over-stated.

A Nation at Risk

* * * * *

These statements are so global that it is useful to look at the data that is causing the concern. Many of the current studies refer to the same basic sources of data, each study giving its own description. The collective result can be the impression that there is more data than actually exists.

International Comparisons

Several of the above statements refer to ways in which the United States is perceived to be losing ground to other countries: productivity, product quality, tech-nological development. Some studies assume that our education is to blame and provide data comparing educa-tional achievement internationally. There is no proven relationship between educational achievement measured by specific tests and international productivity compari-sons, but nevertheless, the following educational compar-isons give pause:

● In international achievement surveys in mathematics (1964) and science (1970-71), U.S. students scored lowest of all 18-year-olds.

● In international comparisons of student achievement (1973-77) using 19 academic tests, American students were never first or second and, in comparison with students from other industrialized nations, were last seven times. American students placed in the lowest third in reading

4

comprehension, lowest in mathematics, and lowest, along with Ireland, in civic education.

One researcher questioned whether America's low standing comes from the fact that a larger proportion of young people attend high school in America than in other countries and therefore had a chance to be tested. (While in the United States about 75% of young people graduate from high school, 45 to 55% complete the equivalent of grade 12 in Sweden, and, in West Germany, where the Oberprimaner goes up to Grade 13, only 15% graduate.) In fact, the top 9% of students in America did as well as the top students in other countries. This suggests the possibility that student achievement scores in other countries might compare less favorably with those in the U.S. if as large a percentage of their young people graduated from high school as do here.

Researchers found a source of comparison in Japan, where high school education is more nearly universal. In fact, 95% of Japanese teenagers graduate from high school, compared with 75% in the United States. As in comparisons with other nations, top U.S. students scored as well as top Japanese students, but (at least in math and science) the remaining 90% of Japanese students did far better than Americans. So it appears that Japan does better than the U.S. both in terms of the percentage of students who graduate from high school and in their math and science achievement.

Many observers, however, point out problems with Japanese-American comparisons. We do not know that education is a causal factor in industrial productivity. Rather, it may be that societal characteristics are major factors in the outcomes of both education and industry. Moreover, even if it were proven that education has a strong influence on productivity, it is not clear that we would want to transplant the Japanese system of education unselectively. Many Japanese are now questioning that system. One reported concern is the large percentage of students (estimated to be as high as 50%) who sit in classes but have trouble following the pace of instruction. Some fear that even students who do succeed academically are under so much pressure that they are affected emotionally. And, ironically, a growing number of

5

Japanese question whether the education system is producing what advanced technology needs: students with imagination and critical thinking skills.

Ernest Boyer, author of High School: A Report on Secondary Education in America, prepared for the Carnegie Foundation for the Advancement of Teaching, gives perspective to international comparisons:

> Behind the meager international data lie values in the American educational system that explain perhaps both our victories and our defeats. Americans have been less awed than many other countries by "high culture." We have been more reluctant to define what it means to be an educated person. And we are deeply suspicious of central control of education and uniform standards, although we yearn for uniform results. (p. 35)

> When viewed in historical perspective, high schools have been, we believe, remarkably successful. These "peoples' colleges"--as they were once called--have educated waves of new Americans, expanded opportunity for historically bypassed minorities, and provided-- for millions--a door to work and further education. Perhaps no other institution has reflected more completely the hopes and aspirations of the nation. (p. 36)

Measuring Ourselves Against Ourselves

Comparisons between the late 1970s and earlier times show substantial declines in student achievement, and these declines have been a major cause of the current alarm.

In looking at declining achievement among college-bound students, the measure most often referred to is the College Board's Scholastic Aptitude Test, which is designed to measure "developed abilities."

The College Board, in On Further Examination, describes the 1963-to-1977 decline:

> ...[a] 49-point drop in the score average on the Verbal part...and a 32-point drop...on the Mathematical

6

part....a decline of this magnitude continuing over a 14-year period, following a previous period of stable or even slightly rising score averages, is clearly serious business. (p. 5)

Concerned observers asked whether the decline might reflect the fact that many more young people were going to college and, therefore, took the College Board tests--a democratic expansion of opportunity. The College Board studied the decline and concluded that the broadening of the test-taking population could indeed explain an early part of the decline, but that a later part of the decline demanded another explanation:

The pattern changed after about 1970. The "compositional" shifts slowed down materially. What showed up increasingly was an across-the-board score decline, the apparent consequence of more "pervasive" changes or influences affecting higher- and lower-scoring groups alike. (p. 13)

The College Board's view of the nature of these influences is presented in the next chapter, where causes of the problems are explored.

The study cautions that SAT scores are a limited gauge, and many educators support their point of view:

It would be too bad...if our concentration on the implications of a decline in the statistical averages on a set of standardized examinations should seem to ignore how incomplete a measure this is of either educational or broader human purpose. (p. 48)

Other comparisons across the decades are made in terms of all high school students, not just the college-bound, and this data shows a decline too. A Nation at Risk (NAR), the report of the National Commission on Excellence in Education, describes the decline and current ability levels as follows:

Some 23 million American adults are functionally illiterate by the simplest tests of everyday reading, writing, and comprehension.

About 13 percent of all 17-year-olds in the United States can be considered functionally illiterate. Functional illiteracy among minority youth may run as high as 40 percent.

Average achievement of high school students on most standardized tests is now lower than 26 years ago when Sputnik was launched. (p. 8)

Much of the data used in comparisons over time comes from the National Assessment of Educational Progress (NAEP), which tests samples of all students at ages 9, 13, and 17 in numerous areas of study. The NAEP, in <u>National Assessment Findings and Educational Policy Questions</u> by Rexford Brown, describes the abilities that show decline, in specific academic fields:

● <u>Reading and Writing</u>:

It would appear...that the vast majority of America's students are literate readers (close to 90 percent) and literate writers (probably close to 75 percent). However, the fact that declines have occurred in inferential comprehension and in more difficult writing tasks should be cause for concern. It would appear that [the]...standard of literacy...10 to 15 years ago is rapidly becoming obsolete. To the extent that analytic, interpretive, and evaluative literacy skills are increasingly demanded by an "Information Society," NAEP findings suggest that there is a growing <u>illiteracy</u>. (p. 3)

The above figures also mean that 10% of high school students are illiterate readers and 25% are illiterate writers. More specific information from NAEP on the nature of the reading and writing problem:

More than a quarter of the teenagers say it is usually hard for them to finish a book they have started.

One-third of the teenagers say it is hard keeping their minds on reading.

Forty to 50 percent of the teenagers say it is hard for them to read materials with "new words."

8

One-third of the teenagers say they have trouble finishing "long books."

One-third of the teenagers have problems finishing classroom silent reading.

When asked to respond to literary works and explain their response in writing by analyzing the work, only 5 to 10 percent of teenagers demonstrated strong analytic skills.

When asked to discuss theme and main idea of literary passages, students tended most frequently to retell the story or poem.

If the characters and situations are close to the students' experience, they respond with a personal analysis...usually undeveloped, unsupported and rather notional (e.g., "he shouldn't have said that to his father," etc. (p. 17)

The percentage of 17-year-olds writing adequate analyses to substantiate their opinions about the mood of a literary work declined 10 percentage points between 1971 and 1980.

...a sizeable proportion of young people--10 to 25 percent--display very serious problems with writing.

...about 20 to 25 percent of the students are fearful about writing, have a sense of doom about it and avoid it whenever they can. (p. 16)

● Math and Science:

There was a steady decline in science achievement of 17-year-olds in national assessments in 1969, 1973, and 1977. The decline in physical science, however, does not appear to be as steep from 1973 to 1977 as from 1969 to 1973, and the decline across the three assessments was less for biology than for the physical sciences.

A publication of the Education Commission of the States (ECS) offered this analysis of students' difficulties in mathematics:

9

Results from the latest NAEP mathematics survey (1977-78) provide evidence that youngsters fail to "think through" problems. For example, about 60% of the teenagers knew that the sides of a square are of equal length, and about half the 13-year-olds and nearly three-fourths of the 17-year-olds could calculate the area of a rectangle given its length and width. Yet only 12% of the 13-year-olds and 42% of the 17-year-olds successfully figured the area of a square when the length of only one side was shown.

Assessment results also indicate that teenagers do not understand the concepts of fractions, decimals, and percents. For example, when asked to estimate 12/13 plus 7/8, only 24% of the 13-year-olds and 37% of the 17-year-olds gave the correct answer of 2. In estimating 250 divided by .5, 25% and 39% of the 13- and 17-year-olds, respectively, correctly answered 500. The largest percentages ignored the decimal point, giving an answer of 50....

Percentages also appear to stump many young people. Only 35% of 13-year-olds and 58% of 17-year-olds could determine what percent 30 is of 60; only 8% at age 13 and 27% at age 17 could calculate 4% of 75. About one-third of the 17-year-olds did not realize that 5% means 5 out of a 100. (Issuegram #6, p. 3)

● Social Studies: In 1976, only 53% of 17-year-olds knew that each state has two United States senators, and one in seven thought the President is above the law. In fact, between 1969 and 1976, scores on knowledge about government in this age group dropped from 64.4% to 53.9%.

From tests...in the middle and late 1970s[,] almost a third of seventeen-year-olds were unaware that the United States and Russia were both rich in natural resources. Two-fifths failed a routine question on the causes of the American Revolution, and almost a third did not know that the legislative branch of government passes laws. (Theodore R. Sizer, Horace's Compromise, pp. 57-58)

● Higher-Order Skills and Basic Skills: After analyzing declining performance, many researchers observed that the

10

decline seemed to come particularly in "higher-order" skills.

Many, but not all, test scores were declining during the seventies, but the phenomenon was not necessarily caused by problems with the basic skills. In fact, findings...point to problems with higher-order skills such as inference, analysis, interpretation or problem solving....analyses of the Scholastic Aptitude Test (SAT) reveal that the greatest declines in that test also occurred among the items testing higher-level skills and state assessments...have been finding the same pattern. (NAEP, p. 3)

● Special Student Populations: The good news is that minorities show real improvements. Action for Excellence, the report of ECS, points out that:

According to the findings of the National Assessment of Educational Progress, there were improvements in basic skills among the lowest-performing 25 percent of students. Black students as a group, and many other historically disadvantaged students, showed actual improvements in their performance of basic tests of reading, writing and computing--which suggests that our efforts over the past two decades...have had real impact. (p. 24)

However, there are still very serious problems, such as the fact that "according to the U.S. Office of Education, forty to fifty percent of all urban students have serious reading problems." (ECS, p. 22)

And for high-achieving or gifted students, there has been a decline in achievement:

...the largest declines occurred in the highest achievement class--that is, among the best students in each assessment." (NAEP, p. 3)

Over half the population of gifted students do not match their tested ability with comparable achievement in school. (NAR, p. 8)

11

Preparation for College

Colleges throughout the country find that they have to provide an ever-increasing amount of remedial instruction. The Ohio Advisory Commission on Articulation Between Secondary Education and College reports that a large number of college entrants cannot read or write at a satisfactory level for college work. The Southern Regional Education Board gives as an illustration the fact that Virginia's colleges estimate that they spent $13 million on remedial education in 1981-82. The National Science Board Commission on Precollege Education in Mathematics, Science and Technology, in Today's Problems, Tomorrow's Crises, gives the following data on the need for remedial work in mathematics:

> Remedial mathematics enrollment at four-year institutions of higher education increased 72 percent between 1975 and 1980, while total student enrollments increased by only seven percent. At public four-year colleges, 25 percent of the mathematics courses are remedial; and at community colleges, 42 percent are. (pp. 2-3)

The College Board's Educational EQuality Project describes in Academic Preparation for College the problems engendered by lack of adequate college preparation (problems apparently not solved by the remedial opportunities available):

> In recent years, many college entrants have not had the knowledge and skills needed for higher education. Many have been severely limited in their choice of college or have been unable to pursue their choice of program. Many inadequately prepared college students have dropped out in frustration or have failed their courses. Many who did graduate had such poor records that they could not go on to graduate or professional study. (p. 1)

Preparation for Jobs

Concern is voiced about lack of educational preparation in the skills needed for both today's and tomorrow's

jobs. In relation to current jobs, <u>A Nation at Risk</u>
reports:

> Business and military leaders complain that they are
> required to spend millions of dollars on costly reme-
> dial education and training programs in such basic
> skills as reading, writing, spelling, and computation.
> The Department of the Navy, for example, reported to
> the Commission that one-quarter of its recent recruits
> cannot read at the ninth grade level, the minimum
> needed simply to understand written safety instruc-
> tions. Without remedial work they cannot even begin,
> much less complete, the sophisticated training essen-
> tial in much of the modern military. (p. 9)

The Education Commission of the States points to data on
problems that would affect performance on many jobs:

A recent survey of 17-year-old students showed that 13%
could not perform reading tasks considered minimal for
functional literacy; 28% could not answer questions
testing literal comprehension; 53% could not write a
letter correcting a billing error; and 85% could not
write a persuasive statement. (p. 22)

To consider preparation for future jobs, some studies
have explored the question of what skills will be needed:

> Due in part to recent advances in electronics and com-
> munications, we live in a society in which service in-
> dustries employ more workers than goods-producing in-
> dustries and in which an increasing percentage of the
> workers will be retrieving, processing, and transmit-
> ting information. The nation's economic emphasis has
> shifted from labor- and resource-intensive jobs to
> knowledge-intensive jobs. Consequently, the skills
> required of many of those entering the labor force
> have changed as well.
>
> The skills many of our nation's workers need include:
> • Analysis and evaluation
> • "Computer literacy"
> • Problem solving
> • Critical thinking and decision making
> • Communication

- Organization and reference
- Ability to synthesize
- Creativity
- Ability to apply concepts in a wide range of situations.

The skills required of some of tomorrow's high-technology workers are those in decline in today's students. (ESC Issuegram #17, pp. 1-2)

Character Development

A number of current studies note that character develop-ment, in terms of traits such as responsibility to the group or empathy, is neglected by the schools. The studies do not give data on the nature or extent of character-related problems. The only reported reflec-tions of the problem deal with specific and extreme manifestations, such as drug and alcohol abuse and violence, and these are reported more as problems for the schools than problems caused by the schools.

The Dropout Rate

A final indicator the studies use to illustrate today's educational problems is the dropout rate; the achievement level of no-longer students could not, of course, even be included in most statistics presented earlier. The National Science Foundation reminds us that 25% of our young people do not graduate from high school.

John Goodlad, in A Place Called School, notes that the dropout rate is still too high, yet he puts the gradua-tion rate in a somewhat encouraging light.

The recent record in increasing the proportion of youths graduating from high schools is particularly impressive. In 1950, only about half of all white and a quarter of all black students graduated from second-ary schools. In 1979, the figures were 85% for whites and 75% for blacks. Also, more young adults have been completing their high school education. In 1970, 75% of adults aged 25 to 29 had finished secondary educa-

tion. By 1979, this figure had climbed to 86%.
(p. 12)

A Case for Educational Restructuring, the report of a
conference at Simon's Rock of Bard College, points out
that the dropout rate affects our population unevenly:

> Forty-six % of the students who enroll in New York
> City's public high schools do not graduate. In the
> inner city schools, this figure increases to 90%....an
> article in the New York Times dated May 6, 1980, indi-
> cated that "over 50% of the children who enter the
> [Chicago] public schools each year leave without
> graduating." (p. 63)

Harold Howe II, Senior Lecturer, Harvard Graduate School
of Education, and former U.S. Commissioner of Education,
described the dropout rate grimly in a speech delivered
to the Education Writers Association: "I would assert
that our republic is in greater danger from the combined
problems of school dropouts and youth unemployment than
it is from academic deficiencies."

* * * * *

In summary, the current problems that are perceived as
outcomes of our educational system are:

● Unfavorable comparisons with other countries; for
  example, the higher educational achievement of
  Japanese students and the implied link between that
  and the higher industrial productivity of Japan.

● Comparison between students in this generation and the
  last in educational achievement--particularly in the
  attainment of "higher order" intellectual skills.

● High school graduates' lack of preparation for work,
  college, or informed citizen participation.

● The number of young people who do not even graduate
  from high school.

The next chapter will present what researchers see as
causes of these problems.

CHAPTER TWO
The Causes of the Problems

Collectively the studies suggest a broad range of factors to explore as causes of the problems. Of these, we focus on those factors that the education community has some chance of influencing and give less attention to factors that educators cannot readily affect (e.g., the effect of women's liberation on the career choices of women who would once have been teachers, the effect of the Vietnam War on young people's view of authority). Suffice it to say that many variables beyond the control of educators affect schools and make the work of educators more difficult.

Readers are warned that the following pages may be discouraging as the chapter explores one problem after another. Bear in mind that there is light at the end of the tunnel: chapters three, four, and five present recommendations for improvement and some examples of approaches that work.

The Number of Hours Students Spend on School Work

Sometimes called "time-on-task," this factor has two parts. One is the number of hours available to a student for classroom instruction, and this part will be discussed below. The second, the amount of time within the classroom actually spent "on-task," will be discussed later in this chapter under teaching methods.

Many observations about the time factor are made in terms of international comparisons presented by A Nation at Risk (the report of the National Commission on Excellence in Education), Educating Americans for the 21st Century (the recommendations of the National Science Board Commission on Precollege Education in Mathematics, Science and Technology), and various publications of the Education Commission of the States (ECS). These studies point out that in many other industrialized countries—England and Japan, for example—the school year is 220 days, compared to our 180, and that within our shorter year, American students spend less time per day learning:

16

our school day six hours, the English eight hours. American students are absent more than Japanese students, and they have less homework than the Japanese two to four hours a day.

Studies maintain that even the hours that American students are in school are not adequately assigned to academic subjects. One study states that Japanese elementary school children spend two-thirds or more of their time on academic subjects, and it implies that in America the time is much less.

Researchers concerned about preparation in mathematics and science discovered that between sixth grade and high-school graduation students in many other industrialized countries take three times as many class hours in science as do the most science-oriented American students. Japanese students average over 26% of their time in mathematics and science over the twelve years of elementary and secondary schooling; the American comparison given is that only 20 minutes a day are spent on these subjects in the primary grades.

The Courses Offered and Chosen

Requirements for high school math and science study are low, 35 states requiring only one year of mathematics and 36 requiring only one year of science; half of all high school graduates take no science beyond the tenth grade. One study claims that not all schools offer adequate mathematics and science courses for talented and motivated students, citing the facts that one-third of U.S. secondary schools do not offer enough math to qualify graduates for admission to accredited engineering schools, only one-third offer calculus, and fewer than one-third offer physics courses taught by a qualified teacher.

The studies do not present much data on courses offered and chosen in academic areas other than math and science. Many studies, however, do discuss electives and take the position that they are increasingly crowding out other curricular choices.

A Nation at Risk notes that in 13 states, 50% or more of the courses required for graduation may now be electives. Enrollment in "general track" programs increased from 12% in 1964 to 42% in 1979, with migration coming from both vocational and college preparatory tracks. (The report does not indicate the proportion from each.) The report takes the position, concurred with by a number of other reports, that general track electives are of less value than more academic offerings:

> Twenty-five percent of the credits earned by general track high school students are in physical and health education, work experience outside the school, remedial English and mathematics, and personal service and development courses, such as training for adulthood and marriage. (p. 19)

> This curricular smorgasbord, combined with extensive student choice, explains a great deal about where we find ourselves today. We offer intermediate algebra, but only 31 percent of our recent high school graduates complete it; we offer French I, but only 13 percent complete it; and we offer geography, but only 16 percent complete it. Calculus is available in schools enrolling about 60 percent of all students, but only 6 percent of all students complete it. (pp. 18-19)

On Further Examination--the 1977 College Board study, chaired by Willard Wirtz--takes a more exploratory attitude toward the value of electives:

> There has been a significant dispersal of learning activities and emphasis in the schools, reflected particularly in the adding of many elective courses and a reduction of the number of courses that all students are required to take. This has been true particularly in the English and verbal skills area.

> In the panel's judgment, any broad condemnation of "more electives" is mistaken. Many of these courses are designed to interest and motivate students.... (p. 46)

> Evidence indicates that the new electives are being taken less by students who are going on to college...

18

than by those who are not. It will have to be determined whether the needs and interests and developed
competencies of those taking these electives are
better met by a course, for example, in Radio/Tele-
vision/Film or an English IV course in the refinements
of the language. (p. 26)

We are inclined to believe, nevertheless, that probably well-intentioned change has reduced the continuity
of study in major fields...[and] has been accompanied
by a tendency to avoid precise thinking. (p. 46)

John Goodlad, in A Place Called School, makes it clear
that although he opposes electives, he believes it to be
important that room be made for careful student choice of
courses to develop individual talents and interests.

Standards for Performance

Many studies point out implicit and explicit lowering of
expectations for the quality and amount of student work.
These studies imply that lower standards result in lower
performance. On Further Examination lists some of the
many ways the message is given:

> ...diminished seriousness of purpose and attention to
> mastery of skills and knowledge...in the schools, the
> home, and the society generally. This takes a variety
> of...forms: automatic grade-to-grade promotions,
> grade inflation, the tolerance of increased absentee-
> ism, the lowering of the demand levels of textbooks
> and other teaching and learning materials, the reduc-
> tion of homework, the lowering of college entrance
> standards, and the inclusion of "remedial" courses in
> postsecondary education. (p. 47)

A Nation at Risk and other recent studies claim that the
emphasis on "minimum competencies," an important thrust
of the past decade, may have helped to lower standards:

> "Minimum competency" examinations (now required in 37
> states) fall short of what is needed, as the "minimum"
> tends to become the "maximum," thus lowering educa-
> tional standards for all. (p. 20)

Content of the Courses

Studies criticize current high school curricula for being too cluttered with facts, too splintered by disciplines, and too narrowly focused on basic rather than higher-order thinking skills.

In Theodore Sizer's view, articulated in Horace's Compromise:

> The load of data purveyed in a typical high school year is staggering. Just because the facts roll out, of course, does not mean that they are either understood or retained.... (p. 94)

> I believe that the qualities of mind that should be the goal of high school need time to grow and that they develop best when engaging a few, important ideas, deeply. Information is plentiful, cheap; learning how to use it is often stressful... (p. 89)

> ...[a] splintered view of knowledge...usually confronts high school students. Their world rarely uses the fine distinctions between academic disciplines. (p. 133)

Goodlad's conclusions are similar:

> Only rarely did we find evidence to suggest instruction likely to go much beyond mere possession of information to a level of understanding its implications and...applications. (p. 236)

> For years, schools and teachers have been criticized for their neglect of the fundamentals. But if our sample is at all representative, it appears that teachers are very preoccupied with trying to teach... precisely what we blame them for not teaching. (p. 243)

In examining specific subject areas, studies again cite the problems of clutter, lack of conceptual structure, and lack of teaching of skills, as well as subject-specific problems:

● English/Language Arts: Goodlad notes an emphasis on
expository writing to the neglect of creative and fic-
tional writing, an absence of attention to the historical
development of words and language, and lack of attention
to the development of listening skills, although students
have to listen a great deal.

Although expository writing may be emphasized above other
modes, many of the studies maintain that it is not taught
for enough time or effectively. Data from the National
Assessment of Educational Progress (NAEP), published in
National Assessment Findings and Educational Policy
Questions, indicates that two-thirds of the 17-year-olds
are not doing any appreciable writing in their classes,
and even in English classes 80% of them spend a third or
less of the time studying writing.

> Only seven percent of the 17-year-olds appear to be
> receiving comprehensive writing training, i.e.,
> training in prewriting, practice in improving papers
> and experience in getting good feedback from their
> teachers. (p. 16)

The Education Commission of the States, in Issuegram #9,
"How Well Can Students Read and Write?," uses NAEP data
to point out that the curriculum still emphasizes instruction in component skills without the application of
these skills. Examples of application include using
writing for generalizing, analyzing, hypothesizing, de-
fending a point of view, elaborating ideas and feelings;
reading ability should include comprehending implicit
relationships established across more than one paragraph
and having strategies for analyzing or evaluating what is
read.

● Mathematics: In addition to the problem cited earlier
of lack of adequate course offerings for talented
students in many schools, a major problem described by
the National Science Board in Educating Americans for the
21st Century, is the outdated content and structure of
the current curriculum.

> At the secondary level there is a need to examine the
> content, emphasis, and approaches....Some components
> in the traditional secondary school mathematics cur-

riculum have little importance in the light of new technologies. The current sequence...can be streamlined, leaving room for important new topics...[which include] discrete mathematics, elementary statistics and probability.... (p. 43)

In addition, Goodlad maintains that teachers rarely go beyond rote teaching from a textbook to activities designed to develop critical reasoning skills.

● Science: Educating Americans for the 21st Century declares an overall need for a drastic reduction in the number of topics covered and more conceptual organization and integration.

In addition to the need to revise the curriculum, many studies note inadequate laboratory facilities. This teacher's statement, quoted by Boyer, illustrates the problem:

> "The saddest place in this school is the chemistry and physics laboratory," said a teacher in one of our field visits...."Chemistry and physics at this school are largely equipment free....there is no single experiment that I can have the kids do, because...the necessary equipment is broken. So we rely on textbooks and work sheets....that's a pretty poor way of teaching science." (p. 295)

● Technology: A subcommittee reporting to the National Science Board Commission on Precollege Education in Mathematics, Science and Technology pointed out that course content is generally nonexistent.

> ...technology is not dealt with effectively now. There are few teachers knowledgeable in technology. Consequently, many teachers are often timid about technical subjects and do not incorporate technology into their lessons. Moreover, there is no provision for including technology in existing courses, and whatever students receive is too little, too late. (Source Materials, p. 69)

● Social Studies: Boyer describes a superficial retracing of the chronology of American history that may not go further than World War I. Goodlad notes that little is taught about the way that heritages and traditions influence the directions and values of society, although, ironically, this is the goal many educators have for social studies. He points out another irony in social studies teaching: the subject is a fertile area for developing reasoning skills, such as "deriving concepts from related events, testing in a new setting hypotheses derived from another set of circumstances, exploring causal relationships, drawing conclusions from an array of data," and teachers list these skills as intended learnings, yet the way teachers test social studies learning is, in contrast, extremely fact-oriented.

● Foreign Language: Goodlad notes an orientation to technical mastery, as shown by short-answer, dictation, or translation tests, and little call for writing original paragraphs or short essays.

● The Arts: Boyer describes as "shameful" the neglect of the arts, in which courses are the last to come and the first to go. Goodlad maintains that the approach is too governed by following the rules and finding the right answer, that music classes are too dominated by rehearsals for events, and that little, if any, emphasis is put on the role of the arts either in learning about other cultures or in personal satisfaction.

● Health: Boyer expresses concern that teaching about health can be found only in mini-units in physical education, biology, and home economics; that such courses offer warnings but neglect healthy living and "wellness"; and that this subject is frequently assigned to physical education teachers who have little background in this field.

● Study Skills: A Nation at Risk articulates what many studies imply throughout: that the teaching of study skills is haphazard, and that, as a consequence, many students enter college without disciplined and systematic study habits.

● Vocational Education: The direction and content of vocational programs are the object of a broad spectrum of criticism. Specialized job training is described as irrelevant or inadequate; Boyer, Goodlad, and Mortimer Adler and his Paideia Group concur that the jobs for which such programs provide training are dead-end jobs that do not merit the use of school time, and that the worthwhile jobs of coming years will take more technical training than the schools alone could provide. The fault is not placed solely on the schools but on a combination of a changing technology and a failure of the schools to keep pace with it. (This criticism has been applied to subject areas other than vocational education, but in vocational education the schools are not expected to be able to keep pace or provide the needed learning facilities on their own.) As The Paideia Proposal expressed the problem, "The techniques and technology will have moved on since the training in school took place."

Several studies note that the problem is compounded by the fact that it is usually minority or disadvantaged students who are assigned to vocational tracks, and thus to limited futures. Goodlad notes as an additional problem that it is close to impossible to change to an academic track midway through high school. He also cites the example of a school where the minority Mexican-American students were disproportionately represented in the vocational track, and he questions whether their frequent assignment to job training off campus (an approach most studies find more realistic than classroom job training) might keep them away from school classes and friends enough to dampen their incentive for continuing their high school education.

● Sports and Other Extracurricular Activities: Opinions differ on the problems. Most of the studies that address these activities, however, are critical of the fact that except in athletics the same small group of students, usually white, confident, and college-bound, participate over and over again, while other students are outsiders. This situation, the studies maintain, is a poor use of school resources. Joan Lipsitz, however, in Successful Schools for Young Adolescents, illustrates that extracurricular activities can surmount this problem.

Sports may not be as vulnerable to the criticism that they cater to elite participation as other extra-

24

curricular activities, yet Goodlad criticizes sports on the grounds that they focus on games requiring sizable teams rather than introducing students to the type of sports that they can enjoy for many years.

The Use of Separate Tracks

Virtually all studies that address the assignment of students of different academic abilities to different tracks cite severe problems with the practice. Boyer discusses the effect on students' self-image and motivation, noting that tracking has a "devastating impact on how teachers think about the students and how students think about themselves." In contrast, he describes a situation in which a teacher gave to vocational track students reading materials that are usually reserved for the academically more able, and he quotes the teacher:

> "I almost cried when I saw them [the vocational students] walking in the halls with their Shakespeare turned so that the whole world could see they were reading Othello." (p. 125)

Goodlad identifies problems more tangible than self-image. In upper tracks, he finds consistently more use of effective teaching practices—more clarity, organization, and enthusiasm—and more focus on higher-level cognitive processes, such as drawing inferences, synthesizing, and making judgments. In classes that are more heterogeneous in terms of abilities, the studies agree that the teaching is more like upper-track than lower-track classes.

Another disadvantage that students in lower-track classes encounter is being in a classroom where the tone is set by a group of students who are, for the most part, unmotivated and have low academic self-esteem.

Students placed in lower tracks turn out to have higher dropout rates, more school misconduct, and higher delinquency. Track placement apparently affects students' plans for the future over and beyond their aptitudes and grades.

25

Again, as with vocational education, a compounding problem is that minority and disadvantaged students are disproportionately represented in the lower tracks. Goodlad sums up the situation with this observation:

> Instead of creating circumstances that minimize and compensate for initial disadvantages in learning, teachers unwittingly create conditions that increase the difficulty of eliminating disadvantage. (p. 164)

Teaching Methods

● <u>Conditions for Active Student Learning</u>: One major criticism is that teachers rarely establish conditions for active student learning. Most researchers are in agreement with Goodlad's conclusion that teaching in the basic subjects "is characterized, on the average, by a narrow range of repetitive instructional activities favoring passive student behavior."

Observers report that during most instructional time students are either being lectured to or are working on written assignments, which usually consist of filling out worksheets. The few questions teachers ask usually seek simple factual information, with less than 1% requiring a response that involves reasoning or an opinion.

In contrast, activities students report liking most--those in which they work actively and with other students, such as role play, interviewing, making things, field trips--receive very little instructional time.

Goodlad notes that there is a gap between the values teachers are taught in education courses, and, in fact, continue to hold, and the values inherent in the activities they choose when they are in the classroom; when in the crunch of the classroom, "teachers resort to practices designed to keep students passive and under control...."

It is worth noting that the studies whose writers have the highest expectations for student achievement are the ones that make the strongest criticism of the current situation and the strongest plea for more active

26

learning. This statement from The Paideia Proposal is a case in point:

> [Students] have spent hours in classrooms where they were talked at, where they recited and took notes, plus hours (often too few) of homework poring over textbooks, extracting facts to commit to memory. But when have their minds been addressed, in what connection have they been called upon to think for themselves, to respond to important questions, and to raise them themselves, to pursue an argument, to defend a point of view, to understand its opposite, to weigh alternatives?
>
> There is little joy in most of the learning they are now compelled to do. (p. 32)

● Teaching Higher-Order Skills: A second criticism, or set of criticisms, of teaching methods is related to the observation that although schools have made good gains in teaching the basic skills, they are doing poorly at teaching higher-order skills and have actually lost ground in this respect in recent years. (Improving basic skills was a deliberate national effort of the last decade, and it bodes well that the effort was successful.) In any case, the new problem is a serious one: researchers maintain that while students, in general, can read, they cannot make inferences from their reading, and, while they can make mathematical computations, they have trouble applying the computations to solving problems.

In an attempt to explain the difficulty in teaching higher-order skills, the studies identify three sometimes overlapping problems with teaching methods. All the studies that address teaching methods note that these problems are aggravated by the time constraints imposed on teachers.

One problem identified is that students are given little opportunity to practice higher-order skills. The studies give different examples of how such opportunity is limited, which include too little chance to write at length, little chance to discuss inferences from reading, and excessive use of multiple-choice tests that require only the recall of specific facts. The 1977 publication On

Further Examination describes a situation that researchers indicate is even more common today:

> ...tests requiring only the putting of X's in boxes
> contributes to juvenile writing delinquency. Students
> learn what they think they need to know. There is
> more than irony in the report of teachers, who used to
> train students to write, now advising them about the
> advantage of using soft-tip pens and pencils so these
> boxes can be filled in more quickly.

> Our...conclusion is that the critical factors in the
> relationship between curricular change and the SAT
> scores are (1) that less thoughtful and critical read-
> ing is now being demanded and done, and (2) that care-
> ful writing has apparently gone out of style. (p. 27)

Sizer identifies as yet another way in which students are
hindered in practicing higher-order skills: the schools'
insistence on the right answer without concern as to how
a student reaches it. Such insistence can "smother the
student's efforts to become an effective intuitive thinker" and "throws away the opportunity to engage him in
questions about his logic and approach."

A second problem hindering the development of higher-
order skills is that teachers and students have little
meaningful intellectual interaction. The NAEP, in National Assessment Findings and Educational Policy Questions, reports lack of even the most conventional type of
feedback: "Sixty percent of the 17-year-olds get neither
written suggestions back from the teacher on their papers
nor discussions with the teacher about their work."
(p. 16)

Goodlad relates lack of interaction to a problem noted
earlier: that students rarely participate actively in the
classroom.

> ...teachers were not responding to students, in large
> part because students were not initiating anything.
> Or when a teacher sought and got a student's response,
> the teacher rarely responded in turn directly to that
> response with supportive language, corrective feed-
> back, or some other meaningful acknowledgement.

Teachers' responses, if any, were more likely to be nonpersonal, such as "all right"--a kind of automatic transition device. (p. 229)

And Sizer suggests that such lack of interaction hinders the development not only of intellectual skills but also of intellectual habits and attitudes:

Save in extracurricular or coaching situations, such as in athletics, drama, or shop classes, there is little opportunity for sustained conversation between student and teacher....and as a result the opportunity of teachers to challenge students' ideas in a systematic and logical way is limited. Given the rushed, full quality of the school day, it can seldom happen ....How one gains (to quote [a] California school's statement of goals...) "the ability to make decisions, to solve problems, to reason independently, and to accept responsibility for self-evaluation and continuing self-improvement" without being challenged is difficult to imagine. One certainly doesn't learn these things merely from lectures and textbooks. (p. 82)

A third problem, perhaps at the heart of all the other problems, is that teachers do not effectively individualize student work, whether it be in verbal instructions or in the tasks and materials students are given. Failure to individualize is at the heart of the other problems; what is wrong with multiple-choice tests, little teacher-student dialogue, and little active student participation is that teachers do not have the opportunity to find out how individual students think, and it is difficult to improve a student's thinking process without knowing what it is.

Goodlad notes that teachers have been urged to "provide for student individuality in learning rates and styles," but that the result is that students work "independently at all levels but primarily on identical tasks, rather than on a variety of activities designed to accommodate their differences," and that "secondary teachers rarely individualized classroom procedures." Goodlad adds that even when kits are used with the intent of individualizing instruction, all that varies is the amount of time expected for different students to complete the work.

29

The Paideia Proposal maintains that many students' deficiencies in reading and writing can be explained by a lack of drilling and coaching. Coaching is described as largely a one-to-one process. (It will be addressed further in chapters three and four.)

● Inept Remedial Instruction: A third criticism of teaching methods is that most schools and teachers are ineffective at providing remedial instruction. This problem, too, is often seen as a failure to individualize, to understand individual learning difficulties and design appropriate instruction. Goodlad notes that remedies such as holding a student back for a year or placing him in a lower track do not work, because the specific learning problems usually go undiagnosed. Proceedings of the Fourth Conference of the University/ Urban Schools National Task Force include the following comment:

> When students fail in reading or mathematics, what typically happens? They are given more instruction in reading and mathematics, often under the guise of "remediation." (p. 44)

The report also offers this description of a situation that existed before a school implemented a program to diagnose missing components of intellectual skills for students having difficulties:

> ...after years of remedial work,...75 students still could not perform because they had never developed the necessary abilities for learning. So long as remediation procedures are targeted to the symptom (failure in reading or in arithmetic), rather than the cause (lack of intellectual skills and thinking competency), then we can predict students will continue their failure to thrive and failure to learn. (p. 44)

Not necessarily blaming lack of individualization, The Failure of Our Public Schools: The Causes and a Solution (National Center for Policy Analysis) questions schools' abilities to provide remedial instruction:

> Some evidence suggests that the public schools have no idea how to teach students with learning problems.

For example, a special summer school session was established in Dallas in 1982 to instruct 1,369 students
who had failed to master minimum skills in reading,
language and mathematics in their regular courses. At
the end of the session, only 10.5 percent of the
students had mastered the minimum skills. The cost:
$900,000 for the program--$6,250 per successful
student. (p. 11)

Finally, the College Board Educational EQualtiy Project
report, Academic Preparations for College, underlines the
seriousness of the problem by stating that teachers must
be aware of a student's learning difficulties in subject
areas other than their own, because inadequate skills in
one area can affect another--for example, reading difficulties can affect achievement in mathematics or science.

● Use of Classroom Time: A fourth criticism of teaching
methods, which is not new to this decade, is that classroom time is not used efficiently. The Education Commission of the States cites the complaint that "poor teacher
classroom organization and management whittle away the
amount of time spent on learning." Since homework
assignments are seen as a way of increasing time-on-task,
another form of this criticism is that students do not do
enough homework. The following statements demonstrate,
however, that not all such time-on-task problems are
within teachers' control:

> ...in a large number of schools, a steady stream of
> assemblies, announcements, pep rallies, and other
> nonacademic activities take up precious time, leaving
> teachers frustrated. At one school we visited, a
> class was interrupted on three separate occasions by
> trivial announcements. We agree with the teacher who
> said in exasperation that "the first step in improving
> the American high school is to unplug the PA system."
> (Boyer, p. 142)

> When reading on their own, most teenagers read for
> less than one hour,...do no homework or less than one
> hour per night,...watch television for more than one
> hour per night: half the 13-year-olds watch three
> hours or more, as do one-third of the 17-year-olds.
> (NAEP, p. 17)

31

• Lack of Character Development: A fifth criticism of teaching methods concerns the lack of methods for fostering character development. Lack of meaningful interaction with teachers is given part of the blame here; as noted earlier there is little time for teachers to challenge, support, or otherwise help develop a student's judgment and attitudes. A second type of opportunity missed, Goodlad maintains, is in students' relationships with each other. Apparently students rarely have a chance to work together, set group goals, divide up labor, help each other; such help is often called cheating.

Teaching Materials and Resources

• Textbooks: Criticisms are diverse and include the observations that textbooks are out-of-date, are too easy as a result of trying to accommodate low student reading levels, are too determined by marketplace economics, and represent too small a part of school budgets. Boyer and Goodlad, among others, maintain that textbooks are over-used--in situations where primary source materials would be preferable.

Concerning level of difficulty, A Nation at Risk describes a study that concluded that a majority of students are able to master 80% of some textbooks before they open the books. It is not clear what this figure means--if it means that good teaching is making textbooks a less primary source of learning, it is not a problem. But it is a problem if textbooks do not offer clear explanatory presentations for back-up use.

Addressing marketplace economies, Goodlad points out that although effective teaching in social studies and science calls for a variety of media and primary source materials, it is more profitable for publishers to market textbooks. Other studies note the stultifying effect on teacher initiative of statewide, or even district-wide, textbook adoption practices.

The Failure of Our Public Schools claims that schools devote too small a portion of their budget to textbooks and other instructional materials, citing a decline over the past fifteen years to the current average of .7% of a

32

school's operating costs, with larger portions of the budget going to increasing labor costs.

Today's Problems, Tomorrow's Crises (a report of the National Science Board Commission on Precollege Education in Mathematics, Science and Technology) notes that most mathematic and scientific curricula were developed over twenty years ago and need to be revised. They add that there are too few curricular materials that convey the importance of science by engaging students in applications or problem solving.

● Laboratory Apparatus: Many studies document a serious lack of apparatus that is up-to-date and in good condition in both science and vocational courses. Today's Problems, Tomorrow's Crises notes the range of conditions that must be remedied for laboratory apparatus to be used effectively:

> Many science courses in schools throughout the country are being taught without an adequate laboratory component or with no laboratory at all. In some cases, laboratory apparatus is obsolete, badly in need of maintenance, or nonexistent. In other cases, such apparatus is not used because of a lack of paraprofessionals or aids to set up and maintain equipment, a condition that has become increasingly important due to the greater concern for safety in the schools. (pp. 5-6)

● Computers: All studies that address the use of computers maintain that their potential use for education has barely been tapped, especially in the areas of mathematics and science.

Conditions of Teaching

Many of the factors held responsible for poor educational outcomes relate to the conditions surrounding teachers' work, including the following:

● Poor Public Image: Many studies note the declining respect for the teacher in America, which Making the Grade (the report of the Twentieth Century Fund Task

33

Force on Federal Elementary and Secondary Education) suggests is part of the decline in respect for all authority figures. In Japan, in contrast, according to Educating Americans for the 21st Century, the status and salary of teachers is higher than that of many other public servants, and 200 science teaching centers are provided for the continued professional development of teachers.

● Lack of Supplies: As indicated earlier, teachers lack up-to-date curricular materials and laboratory apparatus. Apparently, many also lack basic supplies, as suggested by this statement that Boyer quotes from a teacher in an urban school:

> "A lot of times there aren't enough textbooks to go around; the library here is totally inadequate; and the science teachers complain that the labs aren't equipped and are out-of-date. We're always running short on supplies. Last year we were out of mimeograph paper for a month, and once we even ran out of chalk." (p. 158)

● Work Overload and Nonteaching Duties: All the studies that address the workload of teachers agree that it is too heavy, and that it is counterproductive to expect teachers to perform nonteaching duties such as supervising lunchrooms and policing hallways. Boyer lists the daily responsibilities typical of a high school teacher:

> The average high school teacher not only teaches five or six classes a day, but has only 54 minutes of in-school preparation time. Teachers are often responsible for three different levels of a single course. Outside the classroom, teachers must review subject matter, prepare lesson plans, correct and grade papers, make out report cards, and counsel students....Occasionally they are assigned courses for which they are not prepared.... (p. 155)

Goodlad asks how much sensitivity, enthusiasm, and skillful decision making can be expected of teachers working with such an overload:

> Is it realistic to expect teachers to teach enthusiastically hour after hour, day after day, sensitively

diagnosing and remedying learning difficulties? During each of these hours, according to Jackson [author of Life in Classrooms], teachers make 200 or more decisions. During each day of the week, many secondary teachers meet hour after hour with successive classes of as many as 35 students each. As one teacher said to me recently, "It is the sheer emotional drain of interacting with 173 students each day that wears me down." (p. 194)

● Overcrowded Classes?: According to Goodlad, teachers cite overcrowded classes as one of their biggest problems. The 1977 College Board study maintains, however, that pupil-teacher ratios did not increase, but, in fact, steadily declined, at least from 1956 to 1974. The secondary school decline from 21.2 to 19 students per teacher is not as dramatic as the elementary school decline (29.6 to 23), but the ratios at both times are surprisingly low. The study also acknowledges, however, that these are average figures and that there may be many schools in which few classes have fewer than 30 students.

● Difficult Students: Educational Quandaries and Opportunities (a report of the Urban Education Studies project), among others, maintains that there is a small proportion of students in continuous rebellion against the system, who cannot or will not learn, who pose constant discipline problems, and who are, in large part, responsible for teacher burnout.

● Absence of Disciplinary Codes: A number of studies maintain that the lack of clear disciplinary codes in many schools hampers even the most creative and dedicated teachers, and Educating Americans for the 21st Century adds that interpretation of the law often keeps teachers and administrators from dealing effectively with discipline problems.

● The Threat of Violence: According to Boyer, a study reports that 4% of the nation's teachers have been physically abused or threatened and 35% feel unsafe in school. A New York Times poll reports that one-third of New York City teachers and one-fourth of those outside the city had been assaulted. To 40%, violence was a daily concern.

35

• <u>Passive Students</u>: Notwithstanding the data above, and unlike the 1970s, most complaints now are about passive rather than disruptive students. Some studies describe an unspoken agreement between students and teachers in which students sit passively and make no trouble if teachers simply do not ask much of them. In Sizer's view:

> No more important finding has emerged from the inquiries of our study than that the American high school student, <u>as student</u>, is all too often docile, compliant, and <u>without initiative</u>. (p. 54)

Sizer implies that such a student population does not make for a rewarding job for teachers.

• <u>Student Absenteeism and Turnover</u>: <u>City High Schools: A Recognition of Progress</u>, a report of the Ford Foundation, claims that in many of the large city schools high rates of student turnover and absenteeism disrupt learning.

• <u>Work Environment</u>: <u>The Paideia Proposal</u> speaks for many studies in its statement on the quality of the typical work environment for teachers:

> The surroundings in which many teachers work, especially in our large urban schools, would turn any other work place into a shambles. The productivity would drop below the lowest level for survival in business. (p. 57)

Goodlad adds that even lunchtime, under the best of circumstances, does not provide the freedom and relaxation that it does for most workers outside schools.

• <u>Isolation</u>: Most studies paint a picture of professional isolation. Teachers apparently have little opportunity to observe each other teaching, to exchange ideas on teaching with teachers at their own or other schools, to visit other schools, or to work on school-wide or district-wide projects or problems. Three-quarters of the teachers Goodlad surveyed indicated they would like to observe other teachers at work.

Such isolation seems particularly unfortunate in the light of findings which maintain that collegial interaction is a key factor in preventing teacher burnout.

● Lack of Autonomy: Many studies maintain that teachers have little control over the conditions that influence the effectiveness of their work. Boyer lists some of these conditions:

> Teachers do not usually decide how many students and which ones will be in their classes, how long the school day or the class period will be, the format and content of the report card, or even what grades or subjects will be taught. And, in all too many cases, teachers are forced to prepare their students for tests that are unrelated or perhaps inappropriate to the curriculum of the school.
>
> Also, teachers in most settings have little say in the selection of the textbooks they must use. Today seventeen states, most in the South or Southwest, have a centralized system for the selection of textbooks for students in all schools and all grades....At the extreme, in one of the schools...teachers not only were told what textbooks to use, but also were handed a detailed lesson plan for each day. That they lacked much commitment to teaching is understandable. (p. 143)

Goodlad's study of teacher perceptions, however, found that while teachers felt they might not have much control in areas beyond the classroom, they:

> ...perceived that they had almost complete control over selecting teaching techniques and learning activities....a lot of control over setting goals and objectives; use of classroom space; scheduling time and instructional materials; selecting content, topics, and skills to be taught; and grouping students for instruction. (pp. 109-10)

● Salaries: Boyer, Sizer, and A Nation at Risk all maintain that teachers' salaries are so inadequate that many must take other jobs after school hours and during the summer. In 1981-82 the average starting salary for teachers with a bachelor's degree was $12,769, in comparison with $20,364 for computer scientists and $22,368 for engineers. Even after 12 years of teaching the average teacher salary (in 1981-82) reached only $17,000.

● Career Structure: Many studies indicate that not only do salaries start low and rise little with teacher experience, but that in order to achieve reasonable gains in salary or status teachers must leave teaching and enter administration. The best teachers are thus selected out of the profession.

● Basis for Advancement: Studies point out that the basis for career advancement often is not teaching performance. The Failure of Our Public Schools criticizes:

..."medieval guild-type" goals, e.g., the practice of structuring teacher pay scales on seniority or the number of educational degrees instead of on teacher performance, and the policy of granting tenure. (p. 9)

And Making the Grade attributes part of the problem to teacher organizations and unions:

...the organizations--the unions and professional associations--to which teachers belong have protected their weakest members rather than winning rewards for their strongest. They have promoted the principle of equal pay or, at best, a differential pay scale that primarily takes into acount educational background and seniority, thereby limiting the financial incentives available for rewarding superior professional work. (p. 9)

The Teacher Workforce

The studies see as causes of some of our educational problems the quality of the teacher workforce, and this involves both the quality of people who choose to enter and to stay, and their preservice and inservice education. Studies acknowledge that the conditions of teaching, addressed above, may have a strong effect on who can be recruited and what kind of intellectual stimulation

38

they will receive as inservice teachers. The problems cited are as follows:

● Characteristics of Teacher Candidates: A number of studies maintain that not enough able students enter teaching. A Nation at Risk asserts that too many teachers are being drawn from the bottom quarter of graduating classes, and The Failure of Our Public Schools cites poor performance of prospective teachers on minimum competency exams, noting that 38% failed such a test in California.

● Teacher Preparation: Teacher education institutions are criticized by several reports for emphasizing teaching methods at the expense of subject matter and for not imparting the right type of teaching methods. Paideia Problems and Possibilities, for example, maintains that few teachers are trained in either Socratic teaching or in coaching intellectual skills, especially outside the language arts.

● Inservice Training: Many studies note as a problem the general intellectual void in schools, the lack of a feeling that a school is a center of learning for everyone. And they also note the lack of collegial opportunities for teachers to learn from each other. In addition to these issues of environment, the studies point to the fact that no one takes responsibility for updating teachers. Educational Quandaries and Opportunities puts this problem in an interesting perspective:

> It is inconceivable that an engineering firm, hiring a graduate of a school of engineering, would expect that graduate to be able to perform any task in which company staff might engage; or that an accounting firm would expect such behavior from a newly graduated accounting major. Instead, such companies expect to move their personnel through an orderly chain of increasing responsibility; and to provide for additional training, often on company time and at company expense, to facilitate each advancement. But, the analog...does not exist in the schools....school systems ...seem to expect that the graduate of a teacher training institution is de facto able to take over any teaching responsibilities, including for example, a difficult inner-city classroom....schools are simply

39

not funded...to provide the needed additional training or to free the teacher from everyday responsibilities so that the training may be obtained elsewhere. (p. 21)

The need for updating is apparently particularly urgent in mathematics, science, and technology. Boyer quotes a teachers' union official describing the problem:

"A few teachers on the staff will accept [new technology] as a challenge and run the risk of falling flat on their faces as they experiment with it. Do you know what it is like to fiddle around ineptly with a piece of electronic gear before a class of 17-year-olds whose bedrooms resemble the testing laboratories at RCA?" (p. 193)

Educating Americans for the 21st Century agrees with the need for inservice training, citing as inadequate: preparation for teaching about technology, even among certified mathematics and science teachers; opportunities for such certified teachers to be updated in the rapid advances taking place in their fields; programs to certify teachers not presently qualified to teach mathematics or science; district-level supervision to help teachers with pedagogical problems and to provide quality control.

Action for Excellence notes that National Science Foundation summer training programs in mathematics and science, until recently the major source of such training, no longer exist.

• Teacher Shortages and "Out-of-Field" Teaching: A Nation at Risk asserts that despite publicity about an overpopulation of teachers, severe shortages exist in the following fields: foreign language; education for gifted, talented, language-minority, and handicapped students; and, most severely, in mathematics and science.

In many cases, the shortages are alleviated by the employment of unqualified teachers. A Nation at Risk claims that half of the newly employed mathematics, science, and English teachers are not qualified in these areas, and that more than two-thirds of high school physics courses are taught by unqualified teachers.

40

The Need for Quality, a report of the Southern Regional
Education Board (SREB), notes a North Carolina report
that in 1980-81, 37% of teachers of seventh- to twelfth-
grade mathematics were uncertified, as were 30% of
science teachers. In view of such figures, the earlier-
noted lack of training and certification opportunities is
particularly serious.

● Fewer Teachers Entering and More Leaving: The number
of student teachers is, of course, a good guide to
predicting the maximum number of teachers that there will
be in a field. Today's Problems, Tomorrow's Crises
indicates that in science and mathematics, the number of
student teachers has declined seriously ("threefold in
science and fourfold in mathematics"), and only half of
these student teachers actually entered teaching. Of
those teaching now, 25% have said that they plan to leave
teaching in the near future. In 1980-81, 4% of teachers
left for careers in business and industry, a rate
apparently five times the loss from teacher retirement.

● Teacher Burnout: Even when teachers do not leave,
constant stress can impair their performance, a phenomenon called burnout. Educational Quandaries and Opportunities describes the course this problem can take:

> It is clear that many teachers, and particularly those
> in urban systems, suffer from burn-out in varying
> degrees....They no longer believe that they can cope
> with students who confront them in their classes (and
> "confront" is often an apt descriptor!); the name of
> the game, they would say, is survival. Many have left
> teaching...others have simply ceased trying to deal
> with teaching and are content to keep order. And of
> course giving up on students is...a self-fulfilling
> prophecy...students will not learn once teachers have
> decided that they cannot be taught.... (p. 14)

Evaluation and Guidance

Evaluation instruments have many functions in a school.
Problems with the tests that are used for teaching purposes were noted earlier. Boyer is concerned about the
tests used for guidance and claims that the SAT is given

inflated attention considering that colleges currently are less inclined to screen students out. He notes a lack of effective assessment and guidance programs for both college-bound and non-college-bound students who need help in deciding where to go and what to do.

Sizer emphasizes the overload experienced by most high school guidance departments and their contradictory roles as both a place where students come for confidential, personal advice and the disciplinary arm of the school.

Principals

The problems cited for principals center on lack of preparation for the role, the lack of autonomy accorded their role, and their work overload.

● Inadequate Preparation?: Opinions about principals' training diverge. On Further Examination, published in 1977, suggests that even at that time principals were receiving appropriate special training as administrators.

Goodlad, however, maintains that many principals are simply "plucked out of the classroom in June and plunged into the new job soon after." He cites the problems for principals chosen in such a way as the following:

> Few beginning principals know how to prepare a year-long agenda for school improvement; some call faculty meetings only for announcements which could be delivered as effectively on the bulletin board or by a memorandum; very few know how to secure a "working consensus." Current on-the-job training for principals emphasizes their role in instructional improvement. Whatever merit this training may have, it does not usually include provision for developing the principal's capacity to lead in the solution of schoolwide problems. (p. 277)

● Little Autonomy: There is strong agreement that principals do not have the autonomy they need. Boyer describes a situation in which there are five administrative levels above a building principal, each a source of directives. He maintains that principals have limited time and resources, no control over their school budgets (a discretionary fund being a rarity), and little leeway for decision making. "Their ability to reward outstanding teachers, deal with unsatisfactory teaching, or develop new programs is shockingly restrained." This quote from Boyer suggests how hemmed-in principals can be:

"I have no control anymore," says a principal. "We have had five weeks of school, and already fifteen new teachers have come in--and fifteen have left because of bumpings, teachers with seniority removing other teachers. In addition, each year, mostly through inheritance from somewhere else, I get three to five inept teachers." (p. 226)

● Time Overload: The Preparation and Selection of School Principals (SREB) indicates that principals may not be able to spend their time the way they believe they should:

There is substantial evidence that...how principals spend their time does not match...how they feel they should spend their time. A national study of secondary school principals indicates that 83 percent view working with teachers on instructional concerns as their primary responsibility....However, surveys reveal that a very small percentage of a typical principal's week is actually spent in instructional leadership....defined as supervision, teacher evaluation, class visitation, staff development, and material selection. (p. 1)

School Organization

Many factors that constitute the way a school is organized have already been discussed as proposed causes of educational problems--for example, the use of time, arrangement of schedules, allocation of resources. Following are several factors that have not yet been addressed directly:

● Schools That Are Too Large: Many studies maintain that very large schools (one figure given was a school with more than 1,500 students that does not have sub-

43

units) convey a feeling of anonymity, hinder continuity
in human relationships, provide less emotional support,
foster a division between the "insiders" who participate
in many extracurricular activities and the "outsiders"
who participate in none, have more discipline problems,
and have more learning problems going undiagnosed. Joan
Lipsitz, in Successful Schools for Young Adolescents,
suggests why large schools create some of these problems:

> Young adolescents are not ready for the atomistic in-
> dependence foisted on them in secondary schools, which
> is one of the causes of the behavior problems endemic
> to many junior high schools. Behavior problems lead
> to omnipresent control mechanisms, resulting in the
> dissonant combination of an overdose of both unearned
> independence and overbearing regulations. (p. 181)

> Antisocial behavior that results from the randomness
> and brevity of student groupings in most secondary
> schools is substantially reduced in...schools [that
> are organized into small units with continuity over
> time]. (p. 182)

Some studies note the wider range of academic and extracurricular activities a large school can offer, but few
believe the advantages of a very large school outweigh
the disadvantages.

• Lack of Continuity in Human Relationships: A number
of studies describe problems that result from failure to
organize a school in a way that fosters continuity in
relationships between students and teachers, among
students, and among teachers.

Goodlad notes that the brevity of adult-student relationships increase as students move from elementary to high
school, to the extent that some high school students are
not known well by any teacher, and he asserts that:

> [These] circumstances...limit the school's role in the
> humanization of knowledge. At the very time strong
> support systems are required...to keep students' in-
> volvement in school tasks at a high level of interest
> and intensity, these support systems are declining in
> power and variety. (p. 126)

He believes that relationships between students, too, are important, and that they are not helped by the typical scheduling practices:

The never-ending movement of students and teachers from class to class appears not conducive to teachers and students getting to know one another, let alone to their establishing a stable, mutually supportive relationship. (pp. 112-13)

And Goodlad, among others, sees the number and brevity of relationships as taking a toll on teachers:

To reach out positively and supportively to 27 youngsters for five hours or so each day in an elementary-school classroom is demanding and exhausting. To respond similarly to four to six successive classes of 25 or more students each at the secondary level may be impossible. (p. 112)

● Inflexibility of the School Schedule and Space Arrangements: Some studies claim that it is not the length of our school year or school day that is the main problem in use of time, but rather, the inflexibility of the schedule and the ineffective use of time. Boyer presents this view as follows:

The great problem today appears to be the incessant interruption of the bell, the constant movement of students from room to room, the feeling that class is over just as learning has begun....The rigidity of the 50-minute class schedule, for example, often limits good instruction....

The urgent need is not lengthening the school day or school year, but using more effectively the time schools already have—more time to complete a science laboratory experiment, more time to write essays and critique them, more time to engage in extended foreign language conversation. (p. 232)

Sizer points out that frequent changes of room and fellow students give "a frenetic quality to the school day," as well as "tempting opportunities for distraction."

45

Goodlad maintains that the rigid 50-minute schedule makes it difficult to have field trips, small groups, and different teaching approaches; The Paideia Proposal concurs that such 50-minute periods are suitable only for didactic teaching and not for other modes recommended for the development of skills and understandings.

● Lack of Planning for Older Teens: A number of studies observe that schools, at present, are not a good match for the needs of many older teenagers.

Goodlad notes that absentee rates that go as high as 50% of the student body suggest that secondary schooling may be "out of sync" with many of those it is supposed to serve. Meeting the Developmental Needs of the Early College Student, the report of a conference at Simon's Rock of Bard College, raises the problem of "senioritis," which it describes as:

> ...a growing phenomenon in many suburban schools and in some special urban schools. It is characterized by restlessness, boredom, and lack of challenge or motivation and affects a large number of able secondary school seniors or even juniors. There are a number of causes for this condition. A growing number of students have completed or nearly completed graduation requirements by the end of the junior year and are "marking time" waiting for entrance into college. Other students are not motivated by traditional schedules and procedures, and some students with special talents do not find appropriate courses or programs. (p. 19)

● Lack of Opportunities for Service or Character Development: Boyer asserts that although a school can have numerous clubs and extracurricular activities, it is possible for a student to finish high school without having the experience of helping people in need--for example, the elderly or young children.

The School Plant

Studies claim that many school plants are unattractive or difficult to adapt to new recommendations, and some are unsafe. Goodlad writes of the sterile drabness of

46

classrooms that becomes worse as students move up the grades, and he asks why schools do not give as much thought to the effect of environment as businesses do.

High Schools: A Recognition of Progress notes:

> Many schools have rundown physical facilities that are, in some cases, safety and health hazards. The effort needed to overcome such physical deficiencies takes up valuable time and energy that could be better used for teaching and learning. (p. 68)

Educational Quandaries and Opportunities identifies a dilemma for administrators of urban schools:

> Big cities are also older cities, and much of the school plant is also old. School administrators are castigated for not closing antiquated buildings that are...costly to maintain, but are equally castigated should they propose to erect new structures to replace them, especially in view of today's high building costs and declining enrollments....the space that does exist is relatively inflexible, difficult to adapt to...innovations. (p. 13)

Boyer presents a list of the basic repairs needed that suggests the magnitude of the problem:

> A survey of 100 school districts in 34 states showed:
>
> -71 percent of schools need roof repairs or replacements
> -27 percent need repair or replacement of heating and air conditioning equipment
> -20 percent fail fire and safety standards
> -13 percent are not meeting building requirements for the handicapped
> -11 percent have not removed asbestos from buildings
> (p. 293)

Demands and Restrictions of Others

Most studies maintain that schools are being asked to solve too many social problems with too few resources and too many restrictions. The groups most frequently cited as imposing problematic demands are as follows:

● The Public: Making the Grade lists some of the non-academic tasks the public expects of the schools:

> The schools...have had to provide a wide array of social services, acting as surrogate parent, nurse, nutritionist, sex counselor, and policeman. At the same time, they are charged with training increasing percentages of the nation's youth, including large numbers of hard-to-educate youngsters, to improved levels of competency so that they can effectively enter a labor market in which employers are currently demanding both technical capability and the capacity to learn new skills. (p. 4)

To this list of expectations Education Quandaries and Opportunities adds government-mandated programs, and, to make matters worse, the programs frequently change:

> So many new ["revolving door"] programs are being introduced into the schools that a daily computer print-out virtually is needed to keep up. Many of these new programs have been mandated, for example, Title I, mainstreaming, career education. Many are mounted in response to the public's virtually insatiable demand for services.... (p. 15)

> ...these new programs are replacements for or supplements to the previously existing programs. Their adoption carries the implication that the previous programs are inadequate...or that the personnel working in them are ineffective. Resentments are bound to exist....the new programs must be articulated with those older program elements...producing a variety of logistical and resource reallocation dilemmas. ...these new programs are typically supported with outside funds and hence are not subject to cuts or reallocations when fiscal exigencies emerge. Categorical programs thus come to occupy a larger and larger proportion of school curriculum and time. (p. 16)

● Unions: Unions are another source of demands and restrictions, especially for city schools. Educational

Quandaries and Opportunities describes the history of the
situation and the current consequences:

> The big cities have also traditionally been strong
> union towns....The [school] board may well find itself
> having to bargain with from ten to fifteen different
> unions, including teachers, administrators, custodi-
> ans, cooks, electricians, carpenters.... (p. 13)

> In the early years...school systems were represented
> by naive bargaining agents (often a team consisting of
> the superintendent and several board members)....they
> tended to give away too much and to enter into what
> are often now called "handcuff" contracts. Tight
> union contracts tend to militate against the kind of
> creative, self-initiating activity that must charac-
> terize a professional group if it is to function at
> peak levels. Today, even fiscal problems cannot be
> dealt with without carefully differentiating contract
> from non-contract items; virtually every non-contract
> item must be severely slashed before unions will
> consent to reopen negotiations. (p. 14)

● The States: States can be a source of unproductive
demands and restrictions when they create overly specific
education codes. Boyer describes one code that has since
been revised:

> Typical of many states, Texas had a tangle of compli-
> cated, often irrelevant education laws. One section
> of the code, since repealed, required that kindness to
> animals be taught. (p. 290)

● Local Politicians and Interest Groups: Educational
Quandaries and Opportunities describes the type of political or economic interests that frequently affect school-
board decision making:

> Schools became pawns in a variety of power games--in-
> tegration, urban renewal, real estate sales, campaign
> promises of "no new taxes," to name a few. Schools
> are attacked as godless or immoral, and pressures to
> bring their programs into conformity with this or that
> world view are felt every day--sometimes complete with
> book burnings. School board members who view their

49

tenure on the board as a stepping stone to some other
position in politics do not wish to do anything that
might alienate a potential constituent. Vendors who
sell supplies to the schools do not want to see
buildings close and sales disappear. (p. 23)

• Colleges: Ironically, the difficulty usually cited in
the case of colleges is the lack of stringent demands.
Many studies seem to fault colleges rather than praise
them for offering remedial opportunities (except in the
case of minority and disadvantaged students). The
assumption seems to be that high school students will not
achieve their potential unless the college entrance pressure system has no escape valves. The following statement of the Advisory Commission on Articulation Between
Secondary Education and Ohio Colleges on the lack of high
and well-disseminated standards is typical of the position of many state and national commissions:

> Fundamentally, students do not take the college pre-
> paratory curriculum, or schools do not make that cur-
> riculum sufficiently rigorous, because of extensive
> and widespread confusion as to what colleges and uni-
> versities require for admission. While state law does
> permit public universities to require a specified
> preparatory course for admission, the fact is that
> anyone can enter a state college or university, re-
> gardless of the courses taken in high school or the
> record made there. (p. 2)

Funding

How and at what priority level a society should fund its
schools is a fundamental question. We do not address
that issue here; we simply present what the studies have
pointed out as some relatively new funding-related problems that schools are encountering. Such problems include both new drains on funds and the energy schools
have to divert into the current processes for obtaining
funds.

• Inflation: Educational Quandaries and Opportunities
suggests the problems created by inflation:

50

...rising labor costs, and soaring energy prices make
budgets obsolete almost before they are printed. A
significant proportion of the staff in school business
offices is devoted to finding ways to make the dollars
stretch just a few days longer. (p. 11)

Schools find themselves under pressure to husband
their resources more carefully, to become more
accountable, and above all, to be more efficient in
their operations. (p. 12)

And the University/Urban Schools National Task Force
reported on the effect in two cities. In San Francisco
inflation increased 53.2% between 1975 and 1982; in the
same period general funding for the public schools was
increased by only 5%. In New York City the fiscal crisis
of 1976 caused the school system there to lose 11,000
teaching positions and a cut in service equivalent to 25%
of the contemporary budget.

● Declining Enrollments: Educational Quandaries and
Opportunities points out that just at this time, when
every dollar counts, and the amount of money a school
system receives is determined by head counts, enrollment
is dropping. The report suggests that the result may
come to "schools within a system...competing with one
another for bodies since maintaining head counts means
maintaining budgets and personnel."

● Hard-to-Cut Budgets: Educational Quandaries and
Opportunities explains why school budgets can be hard to
cut:

Schools are labor intensive operations; thus, it is
not unusual for 80 percent or even 90 percent of the
budget to be tied up in line-item personnel costs.
There is little "fat" that can be trimmed: Budget
reductions mean personnel lay-offs, and that in turn
produces its own ramifications.... (p. 22)

● Funding Cuts for Needed Programs: City High Schools:
A Recognition of Progress claims that reduction of funds
for programs for students who are disadvantaged, handicapped, non-English-speaking, or recent immigrants, "is
beginning to erode some of the academic gains made when

51

such funds were available." And, just as it has become clear how important teacher skills and morale are for educational improvement, the report notes that:

> Insufficient funds and time to support ongoing teacher development or inservice training erode the instructional strengths of even the best teachers. (p. 68)

● Procedures for Acquiring Funds: Despite the cuts referred to above, many school programs are still funded by federal or state categorical grants, but such funding presents its own problems. Educational Quandaries and Opportunities describes the procedures schools must follow to obtain such grants:

> Elaborate grant proposals are typically required, and the programs must be evaluated and reported....Many of the activities associated with acquiring, expending, and accounting...take on the air of a ritual dance,... not necessarily best designed to cope with local problems....the sheer time and effort involved in carrying out the rituals represent a significant proportion of the resources available. (p. 15)

The Failure of Our Public Schools sees as a problem the direction of funding incentives that encourage schools to channel resources into improving attendance rather than into improving achievement.

Research Input

Educational Quandaries and Opportunities cites as a problem the character of the research available to schools:

> ...research and evaluation offices have not produced very useful data. Often they have limited their attention to scores derived from tests of dubious curricular or contextual validity. Their studies have been more appropriate to the laboratory than...the classroom....they have ignored vast quantities of useful...human and political information, on the grounds of its subjectivity. A false sophistication and pretentious vocabulary sometimes...[makes their reports] next to useless....however,...such behavior

is sometimes...in response to expectations...[of the] Federal government for "objective-scientific" research. (p. 20)

The Situation for Minority and Disadvantaged Students

Throughout this listing of causes of poor education, there are indications that the situation is worse for minorities in almost every area. Some studies explicitly describe their plight. For many minority or disadvantaged students:

Troubled high schools frequently are in inner cities where problems of population dislocation, poverty, unemployment, and crime take priority over education. They also may be found in decaying suburbs or in rural communities racked by poverty and neglect.

Students in failing urban schools often jam into battered buildings with wire-covered windows and graffiti-covered walls. Tile and other hard surfaces reflect the glare from naked light bulbs hanging in protective cages of wire.

Changing classes is like the morning rush hour in Manhattan. Students push and shove in crowded stairways, or ride dangerous elevators and escalators often brought to a quick halt by pranksters. Neighboring residents complain of noise, vandalism, and drugs.

Security guards patrol the halls, attempting to keep order. When violence breaks out, teachers often turn away. They're afraid. On a good day in such a school, the attendance is 50 percent. (Boyer, p. 16)

And for the staff:

The major problem in teaching English in a New York City high school today is the total unreality that possesses our Central Board, the bureaucracy and the politicians.

...we labor under...classes that are in constant flux: numbers that can reach forty; no supplies (paper, pencils, and limited textbooks); a huge range of talents and attendance on the part of the students. Moreover, reading and listening to the media as they report the politicians' criticisms and suggestions is demoralizing. (A New York City teacher, quoted in <u>Proceedings of the First Conference of the University/Urban Schools National Task Force</u>, p. 64)

* * * * *

These, then, are the factors researchers have identified as they search for the causes of disappointing educational outcomes. The next chapter summarizes the studies' attempts to address these factors.

CHAPTER THREE
The Studies and Their Recommendations

> The temptation now is to provide a simple list of
> all recommendations. This I resist. We are
> prone to making laundry lists of unconnected,
> simplistic solutions to complex problems. My
> proposals are not intended to be prescriptive.
> Rather, they are designed to illustrate direc-
> tions and guiding principles for betterment. And
> they are interconnected.
>
> --John Goodlad, A Place Called School

This chapter contains summaries of the findings or recommendations of 33 studies, chosen by the criteria that:

● They make relevant points for local planners.

● Their focus is comprehensive.

● They were conducted under the auspices of experienced
educational institutions.

The studies are varied in method (ethnographic observations, essay, collection of standardized data), in audi-
ence (government agencies, business community, educators), and in focus (description of what actually goes on
in schools, analysis of which practices do and do not
work, recommendations for improvement).

Any summary is a selection. We have chosen to present
those aspects of the studies that are relevant to what
should be done to improve the quality of American education. The summaries do not go into detail on study methodology but provide brief descriptions on the nature and
scope of each project. The information presented in the
summaries was selected from the content of the studies
according to the following principles:

● We selected those recommendations that are relevant
for local planners in relation both to action they can
take and to information they should have about action
others are being asked to take.

• In most cases, we did not preserve the way each study was organized but, for the sake of consistency, used standard categories across the studies.

• We did not always preserve the emphasis of a researcher. If a minor point was unique or seemed especially relevant or feasible, we gave it more attention than the study did.

• We did not always present the full scope of a study; in some instances more attention was given to material that contributes something new to the overall pool of recommendations.

• We did not always preserve the detail. For example, where a study lists recommendations with many subcategories, only the general points may be reported.

• We did not always give space in proportion to the length or likely impact of the study. Several studies that were directed to smaller audiences are given relatively larger play here because they make important points that require full description.

We hope that our effort to make the studies accessible does not reduce them to what Goodlad describes as "laundry lists." We endorse his caveat that the recommendations be read as examples of general directions for improvement and with the understanding that they are interconnected—that improvement along one dimension needs the support of improvements along others in order to last.

The studies are grouped into four categories, and within each category they are sequenced chronologically by the date the study began publication of its research. Following is a listing of the studies by category in the order in which they appear.

STUDIES THAT FOCUS ON RECOMMENDATONS FOR IMPROVING THE EDUCATION OF ALL STUDENTS

The Need for Quality: Southern Regional Education Board

The Paideia Proposal: Mortimer J. Adler and the Paideia Group

National Assessment of Educational Progress: Center for the Assessment of Educational Progress; Educational Testing Service

A Nation at Risk: National Commission on Excellence in Education

Making the Grade: The Twentieth Century Fund Task Force on Federal Elementary and Secondary Education Policy

Action for Excellence: Education Commission of the States

Princeton: A Place for Learning: Princeton Regional Schools

Educating Americans for the 21st Century: National Science Board Commission on Precollege Education in Mathematics, Science and Technology

High School: A Report on Secondary Education in America: Ernest L. Boyer; The Carnegie Foundation for the Advancement of Teaching

A Place Called School: Prospects for the Future: John I. Goodlad

Horace's Compromise: The Dilemma of the American High School: Theodore R. Sizer

An Education of Value: National Academy of Education

Policy Options for Quality Education: National Association of State Boards of Education

The Failure of Our Public Schools: The Causes and a Solution: National Center for Policy Analysis

Education and Economic Progress: Toward a National Education Policy: The Federal Role: The Carnegie Corporation

57

Improving Student Performance in California: Recommendations for the California Roundtable: Berman, Weiler Associates

*Against Mediocrity: The Humanities in American High Schools: Chester E. Finn, Jr., Diane Ravitch, and Robert T. Fancher, editors

STUDIES THAT FOCUS ON RECOMMENDATIONS FOR IMPROVING THE EDUCATION OF COLLEGE-BOUND STUDENTS

On Further Examination: Willard Wirtz; The College Board.

The Advisory Commission on Articulation Between Secondary Education and the Ohio Colleges: Ohio State Board of Regents/State Board of Education

The Educational EQuality Project: The College Board

STUDIES THAT FOCUS ON WHAT DOES AND WHAT DOES NOT WORK IN EXISTING PROGRAMS TO PROVIDE EDUCATIONAL EXCELLENCE

Meeting the Development Needs of the Early College Student: Nancy Goldberger; Simon's Rock of Bard College

The Walls Within: Work, Experience, and School Reform: The Huron Institute

The Effective Schools Movement: Ronald Edmonds

The University/Urban Schools National Task Force: Richard M. Bossone

High School and Beyond: National Center for Educational Statistics

The Project on Alternatives in Education: Mary Anne Raywid

What Makes a Good School?: Gerald Grant

---

*Listed here and briefly described in text; not fully reviewed because publication received too late.

The Good High School: Sara Lawrence Lightfoot

Successful Schools for Young Adolescents: Joan Lipsitz

STUDIES THAT FOCUS ON THE IMPROVEMENT PROCESS

Urban Education Studies: Francis Chase; The Council of the Great City Schools

Redefining General Education in the American High School: Association of Supervision and Curriculum Development

The School Improvement Project: I/D/E/A

The Wisconsin Program for the Renewal and Improvement of Education: Herbert J. Klausmeier; the Wisconsin Center for Education Research

City High Schools: A Recognition of Progress: The Ford Foundation

*Planning for Tomorrow's Schools: Problems and Solutions: American Association of School Administrators

---

*Listed here and briefly described in text; not fully reviewed because publication received too late.

**Studies That Focus on Recommendations
for Improving the Education of All Students**

THE TASK FORCE ON HIGHER EDUCATION AND THE SCHOOLS, organized by the Southern Regional Education Board (SREB) "to consider the linkage between our schools and colleges and...to select those priority issues and problems on which states, schools, and colleges must act jointly in order to strengthen education at all levels." The task force has issued two major reports. The Need for Quality, published in 1981, contains the Task Force's initial findings, recommendations, and some interesting examples of improvement strategies. Meeting the Need for Quality: Action in the South, published in 1983, documents progress since 1981 and offers additional recommendations. Although most of the Task Force recommendations are for state or regional action, others are addressed to or have implications for local planners and are summarized below.

What Should Be Taught

● "...to the extent that society continues to assign superfluous tasks to the schools, the central objectives of education will suffer."

● States should adopt more rigorous requirements for high school graduation.

● "The emphasis on minimum competencies introduces the danger of minimums becoming norms. Concerted emphasis on minimums is necessary to address the failure of some high school students to achieve basic literacy and numerative skills, but the overall concern must be to challenge all students to attain higher levels of achievement."

Vocational Education

● Academic and vocational education teachers must work together if vocational education is going to be successful in teaching academic skills through practical application.

● More effective coordination among high schools, area vocational centers, employers, and post-secondary institutions) is essential.

60

● Occupational programs aimed at preparing students for employment must be related to labor market needs.

Guidance

● Vocational guidance should be a priority; schools should establish links with business and industry to inform this guidance.

Special Populations

● Districts should establish communication with local colleges to design creative programs for gifted students.

● "The commitment to quality...must address the special needs of black students, many of whom have major deficiencies in academic skills. For example, at the college level, a response does not lie simply in denying admission to underprepared blacks, although higher admission standards may be in order over the long term. A permanent solution must involve curriculum reform at the secondary and college levels, with mandatory intensification of communication and quantitative coursework. To a considerable degree, the success of such reform depends on an adequate supply of highly qualified black teachers. Incentives are needed to attract high achievers among the black college students into teacher education programs."

Teachers

● Salary levels should be raised and financial incentives made available for outstanding teaching and relevant graduate education. (This recommendation is developed further in both of SREB's reports in the form of state and district plans for career ladders.)

● With proper safeguards, graduates without education certification (e.g., college and industry personnel) should be allowed to teach in high schools.

Principals

● "The role...should be delineated and the school's organization structured so that the principal can function as instructional leader."

61

● The realistic interpretation of this role may be that of establishing school goals and climate rather than directly influencing classroom practice.

● Authority should be returned to principals through school-based management.

● Districts should develop objective plans for principal selection involving both assessment of behaviors that characterize successful principals and internships for candidates.

● Inservice programs should use local resources of colleges and agencies in individualized programs based on strengths and weaknesses of individual administrators.

* * * * *

Cornett, Lynn M. The Preparation and Selection of School Principals. Atlanta: Southern Regional Education Board, 1983. 16 pp. $3.00

Galambos, Eva C. Issues in Vocational Education. Atlanta: SREB, 1984. 36 pp. $3.00

Meeting the Need for Quality: Action in the South. Atlanta: SREB, 1983. 30 pp. $3.00

The Need for Quality: A Report to the Southern Regional Education Board by the Task Force on Higher Education and the Schools. Atlanta: SREB, 1981. 28 pp. $3.00

Performance-based Pay for Teachers. Atlanta: SREB, 1983. 4 pp.

Southern Regional Education Board, 1340 Spring Street NW, Atlanta, GA 30309

THE PAIDEIA PROPOSAL, by Mortimer J. Adler, on behalf of the members of the Paideia Group, 1982. The Greek word "paideia" means the upbringing of a child; the Paideia Group uses it to signify "the general learning that should be the possession of all human beings." The group's purpose is to design a single course of study for grades 1 through 12 to improve the quality of elementary and secondary education. The group had extensive discussions over three years, published its first recommendations in The Paideia Proposal, and was among the first to open the dialogue of the 1980s on what should be taught in American schools. A second volume, Paideia Problems and Possibilities (1983), discusses questions about implementation. A third volume, The Paideia Program (forthcoming, Fall, 1984), will discuss each element in the curricular framework in detail.

Dr. Adler emphasizes that while the framework is designed for all students, the specifics are to be selected so that they are appropriate for students and their community. He describes Paideia's goals as follows:

● Schooling should foster students' personal growth (mental, moral, and spiritual) and should prepare them to take advantage of every opportunity society offers.

● Schooling should prepare students to be enfranchised citizens by inculcating "civic virtues," and by teaching them the fundamental principles of our government and the duties and responsibilities of citizenship.

● Schooling should prepare students to earn a living by giving them the basic skills that are common to all work.

What Should Be Taught

To allow intense concentration on the course of study, Adler recommends the elimination of all nonessential school activities and all training for specific jobs.

The course of study proposed by the Paideia Group is presented in a chart and described as follows:

The diagram...depicts in three columns three distinct modes of teaching and learning, rising in...difficulty from the first to the twelfth year. All three modes are essential to the overall course of study.

These three columns are interconnected....The different modes of learning...and the different modes of

63

teaching...correspond to three different ways in which the mind can be improved—(1) by the acquisition of organized knowledge; (2) by the development of intellectual skills; and (3) by the enlargement of understanding, insight, and aesthetic appreciation. (p. 22)

	COLUMN ONE	COLUMN TWO	COLUMN THREE
Goals	ACQUISITION OF ORGANIZED KNOWLEDGE	DEVELOPMENT OF INTELLECTUAL SKILLS – SKILLS OF LEARNING	ENLARGED UNDERSTANDING OF IDEAS AND VALUES
	by means of	by means of	by means of
Means	DIDACTIC INSTRUCTION LECTURES AND RESPONSES TEXTBOOKS AND OTHER AIDS	COACHING, EXERCISES, AND SUPERVISED PRACTICE	MAIEUTIC OR SOCRATIC QUESTIONING AND ACTIVE PARTICIPATION
	in three areas of subject-matter	in the operations of	in the
Areas Operations and Activities	LANGUAGE, LITERATURE, AND THE FINE ARTS MATHEMATICS AND NATURAL SCIENCE HISTORY, GEOGRAPHY, AND SOCIAL STUDIES	READING, WRITING, SPEAKING, LISTENING CALCULATING, PROBLEM-SOLVING OBSERVING, MEASURING, ESTIMATING EXERCISING CRITICAL JUDGMENT	DISCUSSION OF BOOKS (NOT TEXTBOOKS) AND OTHER WORKS OF ART AND INVOLVEMENT IN ARTISTIC ACTIVITIES e.g., MUSIC, DRAMA, VISUAL ARTS

THE THREE COLUMNS DO NOT CORRESPOND TO SEPARATE COURSES, NOR IS ONE KIND OF TEACHING AND LEARNING NECESSARILY CONFINED TO ANY ONE CLASS

● Subject Areas:

Language, literature, and the fine arts include grammar, syntax, forms of discourse, some history of English, and comparison to other languages and to a "language" such as math.

Mathematics extends from simple arithmetic to at least one year of calculus, integrating use of calculators from the very beginning and leading to introductory computer use and programming.

Natural sciences include physics, chemistry, and biology, with emphasis on their connectedness.

<u>History and geography</u> include knowledge of human and social affairs nationally and in the world.

The learning activity in a subject area includes not only the knowledge from column one but also the skills and understandings from columns two and three. For example, civics would include (column one) knowledge developed through "didactic instruction in history and the growth of social institutions, a comparative study of which will include and emphasize the institutions of our own country...," and (column three) understanding developed through "seminars in which students read and discuss the Declaration of Independence, the Constitution...,the <u>Federalist Papers</u>,...<u>Democracy in America</u> by Alexis de Tocqueville, and Lincoln's Gettysburg Address..." thereby developing "understanding of such ideas as liberty, equality, justice, rights, property, constitutional government, citizenship, and democracy...."

● <u>Skills:</u> Column two lists the skills to be learned: reading, writing, speaking, listening, observing, measuring, estimating, and calculating; the skills are the backbone of schooling and are necessary for all other learning.

● <u>Understandings</u>: Column three involves values and appreciation and can be approached only through intensive study of individual works through Socratic questioning and participative experiencing.

● Important auxiliary areas are:

Physical education, accompanied by health instruction.

Manual activities, in which boys and girls participate in "typing, cooking, sewing, wood- and metalworking, crafts using other materials, automobile driving and repair, maintenance of electrical and other household equipment...."

Preparation for a career should include an introduction "to the wide range of human work—the kinds of occupations and careers, their significance and requirements, their rewards and opportunities."

Foreign language, to be studied for four to six years, or for long enough to assure competence aimed not so much at usage as at improving skill in the language arts.

Methods

All genuine learning is active, not passive. It involves the use of the mind, not just the memory. It is a process of discovery, in which the student is the main agent, not the teacher.

How does a teacher aid discovery and elicit the activity of the student's mind? By inviting and entertaining questions, by encouraging and sustaining inquiry, by supervising helpfully a wide variety of exercises and drills, by leading discussions, by giving examinations that arouse constructive responses, not just the making of check marks on printed forms. (p. 50)

Three teaching methods, each designed to stimulate one of three forms of learning, are a principal focus of Paideia:

● Telling for Knowledge: Where "information and organized knowledge can be acquired from textbooks or manuals, teachers help such learning...by drills, exercises, and tests...[and by] didactic instruction, that is, lecturing: by telling, explaining, or pointing out the difficulties to be overcome, the problems to be solved, the connections and conclusions to be learned."

● Coaching for Skills: A coach helps the learner to go through the right motions, in the right sequence. He corrects mistakes again and again and asks a student to repeat performance until it is perfected. The coach needs to give some individual attention and can usually do this with groups if the groups are small enough. Extended time is often needed for coaching, and after-school time may be required. Any homework required must be carefully corrected by the teacher.

● Discussion for Understanding: The third kind of learning is the development of greater understanding. The teacher teaches by asking—not telling—and by using materials other than textbooks or manuals. In discus-

sions, students must both ask and answer questions. "The
teacher must be keenly aware of the ways in which insights occur to enlarge the understanding--ways that
differ from individual to individual. That demands close
attention to what is happening in the student's mind as
he or she asks or answers questions, and as one question
or answer leads to another."

Materials and Media

Computer-assisted teaching is a cost-effective aide to
coaching and drilling for the development of skills.
Tapes can help foreign-language teaching.

Video tapes can also help development of knowledge by
occasionally making available effective and engaging
lectures. "The classroom teacher is then free to
concentrate on questions, discussions, and on individual
instruction where needed.

Evaluation

> Written tests...must shift their focus from emphasis
> on verbal memory and the guesswork that is encouraged
> by true-false and multiple choice tests, to an empha-
> sis on the possession of organized knowledge...on
> demonstrable linguistic and mathematical skills; and
> on the power to understand, think, and communicate.

> [Such learning] cannot be assessed by machine-graded
> tests. Essays must be written and must be read....
> Mathematical reasoning must be tracked. Thinking and
> understanding require oral examinations among other
> tests. (II, p. 52)

Special Student Populations

● The improved quality of the Paideia curriculum makes
special programs for the specially gifted unnecessary.

● Programs should be devised to help students with
learning disabilities to function in the common course of
study. Coaching is one method to be employed in teaching
less able learners.

67

School Organization

• <u>Age</u>: Some children can begin school at four, none should begin later than six; on the average, the full course of schooling should take 12 years, but it can vary from 10 to 14 years.

• <u>Groupings</u> should be based on achievement of skills, not solely on age, particularly in classes developing knowledge and skills. In areas such as physical development, manual training, or seminars devoted to understanding of particular works, age-grouping may be important for social as well as educational reasons.

• <u>Tracking</u>: The Paideia Group proposes a one-track program. The program must not be watered down to adjust to individual differences; rather, children whose deficiencies prevent adequate performance must be given special help to overcome these deficiencies.

• <u>Teacher-Student Ratio, Time, and Space</u>: The three different modes of teaching have different sets of requirements:

<u>Didactic teaching</u> can be done well in a class of 35 or 40, in a large lecture hall or laboratory theater, or with closed-circuit television presenting lectures by teachers not on the school's staff.

<u>Coaching</u> cannot be done well with more than ten students and will be more successful with even fewer. The coach should be able to move around the small group of students whose performance he or she is supervising, directing, and correcting, and the students should all be in the immediate vicinity. Time available may have to be longer than the usual 45- to 50-minute period.

<u>Socratic teaching</u> should be seminar style with 20 to 25 students. Such teaching often requires more than a 50-minute class period and calls for a room in which the participants sit around a table instead of in rows. The teacher should be one of the participants, not the performer in front of the group. Having two leaders can enliven a discussion.

● Extracurricular Activities: Activities such as debating teams, school newspapers, and athletic events have some educational merit. "Debating is a good exercise in putting together and expressing coherent arguments. Both writing and business acumen can be sharpened by work on a school newspaper. In addition to physical fitness and skill, athletics, if well supervised, can develop traits of character such as self-discipline, stamina, personal courage, and team spirit. On these grounds, such activities can serve as supplements and reinforcements in a Paideia progam."

Paideia course work should be scheduled during morning and early afternoon, and optional extracurricular activities scheduled later in the day. Financial resources should not be diverted to supplementary activities.

Teachers

● Should have a general college education before specialized training.

● Should show "competence as learners...and...motivation to carry on learning while engaged in teaching."

Principals

● Should be competent and dedicated teachers, with much classroom experience, and should be primarily the head teacher.

● Should administer all school activities to facilitate the main business of teaching. The principal does not have to actually teach but must provide the educational leadership.

Parents

● Must support homework by providing a conducive environment and seeing that it is done effectively.

* * * * *

Adler, Mortimer J. The Paideia Proposal: An Educational Manifesto. New York: Macmillan, 1982. 84pp. $2.95

_____. Paideia Problems and Possibilities: A Considera-
tion of Questions Raised by The Paideia Proposal. New
York: Macmillan, 1983. 113pp. $3.95

_____. The Paideia Program. New York: Macmillan,
forthcoming, Fall 1984.

The Institute for Philosophical Research, 101 East
Ontario Street, Chicago, IL 60611

NATIONAL ASSESSMENT OF EDUCATIONAL PROGRESS (NAEP), an
ongoing survey of the knowledge, skills, understandings,
and attitudes of American students. It is administered
by the Center for the Assessment of Educational Progress
of the Educational Testing Service and is funded by the
National Institute of Education. The NAEP collects and
reports data in several learning areas (reading/litera-
ture, writing, mathematics, science, career and occupational development, citizenship/social studies, art, and
music) at three age levels (9, 13, and 17 years, and occasionally, young adults aged 26 to 35). Publications of
the NAEP include summaries of each assessment, "Objective
Booklets" that define educational goals in most of the
learning areas, and exercise sets that educators can use
to make their own evaluation of student abilities and
achievements.

A recent paper relevant to issues raised by current
studies is National Assessment Findings and Education
Policy Questions, by Rexford Brown. According to Brown,
NAEP research suggests that the decline in student
achievement scores during the 1970s was not caused so
much by lack of basic skills as by lack of competence in
the "higher-order skills such as inference, analysis,
interpretation or problem solving."

Brown recommends that educators "redefine the goals of
education as encompassing more than 'basics' or minimum
competencies," and suggests the following:

● Integrate the higher-order skills into programs
designed to teach the basic skills.

● Require student writing, not only in English classes, but in other subject areas as a way of promoting analytical, interpretive, and evaluative skills.

● Give feedback on student writing.

● Require student rewriting in response to feedback.

● "Stress inferential as well as literal comprehension skills" in reading and literature.

● Encourage students to read and keep them reading for longer periods of time.

● Have students write about their reading in responses that are more than quick and superficial.

● Let students do their own hard thinking. "Some studies suggest that many writing teachers make the hard organizational and structural decisions for their students, leaving the students to 'fill in blanks.'"

● In science and mathematics, "do not wait until students have mastered computation skills before going on to problem solving. Both can be taught at the same time."

Brown supports continuation of special programs to aid disadvantaged and minority students who, despite recent advances, "remain, as a group, below national levels of achievement." But he also states that attention should be paid to "the best students," as NAEP data shows that while the achievement of disadvantaged and minority students has improved over the last decade, "the largest decline occurred in the highest achievement class--that is, among the best students in each assessment."

* * * * *

Brown, Rexford. National Assessment Findings and Educational Policy Questions. Princeton, N.J.: National Assessment of Educational Progress, 1982. 22pp. $3.50

NAEP Newsletter. Princeton, N.J.: NAEP, quarterly. Single copies free.

Selected Publications from the National Assessment of Educational Progress. Princeton, N.J.: NAEP, 1983.

The National Assessment of Educational Progress, Box 2923, Princeton, NJ 08541

A NATION AT RISK: THE IMPERATIVE FOR EDUCATIONAL REFORM, the report of the National Commission on Excellence in Education, chaired by David P. Gardner, President of the University of California. The Commission was created in August 1981 by the Secretary of Education to examine the quality of education in the United States in response to "the widespread public perception that something is seriously amiss in our educational system." It commissioned papers, held public hearings, reviewed existing studies as well as communications from experts and lay people, and surveyed notable approaches to education around the country. The report, issued in April 1983, contained a statement on the condition of education in the United States, as well as recommendations for improvement.

What Should Be Taught

• Standards should be raised and graduation requirements strengthened so that at a minimum students have a foundation in the "Five New Basics" of English, mathematics, science, social studies, and computer science.

English: Four years, equipping students to:
- Comprehend, interpret, evaluate.
- Write well-organized, effective papers.
- Listen effectively and discuss ideas intelligently.
- Know our literary heritage, how it enhances imagination and ethical understanding, how it relates to modern customs, ideas, and values.

Mathematics: Three years, equipping students to:
- Understand geometric and algebraic concepts.
- Apply math in everyday situations.
- Estimate, approximate, measure, and test the accuracy of their calculations.
New, demanding math curricula must be developed for non-college-bound students.

72

Science: Three years, introducing:
- The concepts, laws, and processes of physical and biological sciences.
- The methods of scientific inquiry and reasoning.
- The application of science to everyday life.
- The social and environmental implications of scientific and technological development.
Science courses must be revised and updated for all students.

Social Studies: Three years, enabling students to:
- Fix their places and possibilities within the larger social and cultural structure.
- Understand the broad sweep of ancient and contemporary ideas that have shaped our world.
- Understand the fundamentals of our economic and political systems.
- Grasp the difference between free and repressive societies.

Computer Science: One-half year, in which students come to understand the computer and learn to use it in other Basics and for personal and work-related purposes.

● In addition to the Five New Basics:

Foreign Language: Proficiency usually takes four to six years of study so should be started in elementary school. College-bound students should have two additional years in high school. Such proficiency is important because it "introduces students to non-English-speaking cultures, heightens awareness...of one's native tongue, and serves the Nation's needs in commerce, diplomacy, defense, and education."

The curriculum should offer "programs requiring rigorous effort in subjects that advance students' personal, educational, and occupational goals, such as the fine and performing arts and vocational education." It should also provide instruction in effective study and work skills.

Methods and Materials

● More homework should be required.

● More time should be made available for learning by improved classroom management and organization of the school day.

● Codes of student discipline should be developed that decrease the need for teachers to take time for disciplinary matters.

● Textbooks and other "tools of learning and teaching" should be improved to reflect a more rigorous content as well as the most current scholarship and applications of technology available.

School Organization

● Significantly more time should be devoted to learning the New Basics. This will require more effective use of the existing school day and consideration of expanding to a seven-hour school day and a 200- to 220-day school year.

● Additional time should be provided for gifted or slow learners and others needing instructional diversity.

● Attendance policies should use clear incentives and sanctions to reduce absenteeism and tardiness.

● Administrative burdens on teachers and administrative intrusions into classroom time should be reduced.

● Students should be placed, grouped, promoted, and graduated by academic progress rather than age.

Guidance and Evaluation

● "Grades should be indicators of academic achievement so they can be relied on as evidence of a student's readiness for further study."

● Standardized achievement tests should be used at major transition points for evaluating student progress, identifying needs for remedial or accelerated work, and guidance for work and college.

74

Teachers

Several proposals are offered to improve the quality and
conditions of teaching, as follows:

● A high level of teacher competence in both teaching
and subject matter.

● Competitive, performance-based salaries.

● An eleven-month contract, to allow for curricular and
professional development and development of programs for
students with special needs.

● A career ladder for teachers.

● Reduction of the shortage of science and mathematics
teachers by allowing qualified nonteachers to teach in
these areas, as well as by more programs to train and
retrain teachers in these fields.

● Fiscal incentives to attract outstanding students into
teaching.

● The involvement of master teachers (the highest rung
on the career ladder) in the design of teacher education
programs and the supervision of new teachers.

In a concluding statement A Nation at Risk takes an
encouraging perspective on our national capacity for
educational reform:

> The American educational system has responded to pre-
> vious challenges with remarkable success. In the 19th
> century our land-grant colleges and universities pro-
> vided the research and training that developed our...
> natural resources and...rich agricultural bounty....
> From the late 1800s through mid-20th century, American
> schools provided the educated workforce needed to seal
> the success of the Industrial Revolution and to pro-
> vide the margin of victory in two world wars. In the
> early part of this century and continuing to this very
> day, our schools have absorbed vast waves of immi-
> grants and educated them and their children to produc-
> tive citizenship. Similarly, the Nation's Black col-

leges have provided opportunity...to the vast majority
of college-educated Black Americans.

More recently, our institutions of higher education
have provided the scientists and skilled technicians
who helped us transcend the boundaries of our planet.
In the last 30 years, the schools have been a major
vehicle for expanded social opportunity, and now graduate 75 percent of our young people from high school.
Indeed, the proportion of Americans of college age
enrolled in higher education is nearly twice that of
Japan and far exceeds other nations such as France,
West Germany, and the Soviet Union. Moreover, when
international comparisons were last made a decade ago,
the top 9 percent of American students compared favorably in achievement with their peers in other
countries.

In addition, many large urban areas in recent years
report that average student achievement in elementary
schools is improving. (pp. 33-34)

* * * * *

A Nation at Risk: The Imperative for Educational Reform.
Washington, D.C.: National Commission on Excellence in
Education, U.S. Department of Education, 1983. 65 pp.
$4.50

Available from Superintendent of Documents, U.S. Government Printing Office, Washington, D.C. 20402.

MAKING THE GRADE, issued in 1983 by the Twentieth Century
Fund Task Force on Federal Elementary and Secondary Education Policy chaired by Robert Wood. The task force proposes two general goals for education. For our economic
well-being, education must "ensure the availability of
large numbers of skilled and capable individuals without
whom we cannot sustain a complex and competitive economy." For our political system, "each citizen should have
the capacity to participate fully in our political life;
to read newspapers, magazines, and books; to bring a
critical intelligence to television and radio; to be

capable of resisting emotional manipulation and of setting events within their historical perspective; to
express ideas and opinions about public affairs; and to
vote thoughtfully--all activities that call for literacy
in English."

Making the Grade recommends:

● A core curriculum that provides to all students the
basic skills of reading, writing, and calculating;
technical capability in computers; training in science
and foreign languages; and knowledge of civics.

● Improvements in the teaching environment that would
attract more capable people to the profession.

Other recommendations are directed toward federal education policy and are presented here to inform local planners of what the federal government is being asked to do:

● Emphasize the need for better schools and a better
education for all young Americans.

● Establish and fund a Master Teacher Program to recognize and reward excellent teaching.

● Recognize that the most important objective of
American education is the development of literacy in
English.

● Transfer federal funds now going to bilingual programs
to programs designed to teach non-English-speaking children to speak, read, and write English.

● Support actions that would give public school students
the opportunity to learn in a second language.

● Emphasize "programs to develop basic scientific literacy among all citizens and to provide advanced training
in science and mathematics for secondary school students."

● Continue support for special education programs for
the poor and handicapped.

● Fund any educational programs that are required by the federal government.

● Redirect impact aid so that more is channeled to school districts that are overburdened by large numbers of immigrant children.

● Give attention and assistance "to depressed localities that have concentrations of immigrant and/or impoverished groups as well as those that are already making strong efforts to improve their educational performance."

● Support educational research, especially:
- "The collection of factual information about various aspects of the education system...."
- "The collection of information about the educational performance of students, teachers, and schools...."
- "Evaluation of federally sponsored education programs."
- "Fundamental research into the learning process."

● Establish "special federal fellowships for [children who have not been able to learn in the present system] which would be awarded to school districts to encourage the creation of small individualized programs staffed by certified teachers and run as small-scale academies."

* * * * *

Making the Grade: Report of the Twentieth Century Fund Task Force on Federal Elementary and Secondary Education Policy. New York: The Twentieth Century Fund, 1983. 174 pp. $6.00

The Twentieth Century Fund, 41 East 70th Street, New York, NY 10021

ACTION FOR EXCELLENCE, a report by the Task Force on Education for Economic Growth, Education Commission of the States (ECS), 1983. ECS was established to support the states in their education role. Concerned about the lack of student preparation for the high-technology employment needs of our society, ECS appointed a task force of governors, legislators, corporate chief executive officers, school board members, local leaders, scientists, and educators to determine the job needs of coming decades and how to educate students for these needs. The resulting recommendations are published in Action for Excellence.

ECS also produces Issuegrams that describe approaches to many of the current recommendations for school improvement. The Issuegrams present a variety of findings for policy makers to consider; their findings are not necessarily endorsed by ECS. This summary draws on both Action for Excellence and relevant Issuegrams. The following excerpt from Issuegram #17 gives a rationale and conclusions about the skills that will be needed in future jobs:

> ...we live in a society in which service industries employ more workers than goods-producing industries and in which an increasing percentage of the workers will be retrieving, processing, and transmitting information. The nation's economic emphasis has shifted from labor- and resource-intensive jobs to knowledge-intensive jobs. Consequently, the skills required of many of those entering the labor force have changed as well.
>
> The skills many of our nation's workers need include: analysis and evaluation, computer literacy, problem solving, critical thinking and decision making, communication, organization and reference, ability to synthesize, creativity, ability to apply concepts in a wide range of situations." (pp. 1-2)

What Should Be Taught

● Upgrade the concept of basic skills in all courses to include "learning-to-learn" skills, because most jobs will require not only basic skills but the ability to acquire new ones. These higher-order skills include summary, application, synthesis, problem solving, implication, inference, and creativity.

● "Teaching of problem solving or analytic skills and of more basic knowledge and skills should proceed simultaneously....the learning of more advanced skills should

79

reinforce the learning of more basic skills and provide meaning for their application."

• Devote more time to reading and writing "through practice with increasingly difficult communications tasks set across a variety of content areas."

• ECS supports the academic competencies proposed by the Educational EQuality Project (reading, writing, speaking and listening, mathematics, reasoning, and studying) and adds to them more specific scientific competencies, basic employment competencies, economic competencies, and computer literacy competencies.

• Reduce the number of electives and the credit given for nonacademic courses. Require more academic courses and encourage coherence in sequence of courses.

• Strengthen math and science requirements and add computer science and programming.

• Require speaking and reading literacy in a foreign language.

Methods

In addition to recommending increased howework at all levels, ECS presents research findings about effective teaching and classroom management practices.

• Focus teaching and curriculum selection on the basic skills or agreed-upon academic focus of the school, maintain a fast pace, and cover content extensively.

• Maintain a high student success rate especially for the introduction of new content, classroom work, and homework. "Challenging" students with difficult work for which the success rate is low generally is not effective.

• Monitor individual student performance, praise correct answers, and provide individual, specific, academically oriented corrective feedback on incorrect answers.

• Have a well-organized classroom that includes training students in classroom procedures and transition processes, and a clear, fair, and uniform disciplinary system.

Materials and Technology

● Upgrade the standards for textbooks.

● Use computers when appropriate to supplement the teaching process.

● Apply stringent quality standards to selecting computer software.

● Provide guidelines for selecting appropriate hardware. An "Apple" in every classroom is neither appropriate nor cost-effective.

Evaluation and Guidance

● Monitor performance by a system tied to the instructional program.

Teachers

● Require more rigorous training that provides the skills to teach problem solving and critical thinking and includes an internship period.

● Focus inservice training on effective teaching techniques, and train or retrain senior teachers in current math, science, and computer science.

● Put teachers in control of the classroom improvement process.

● Improve working conditions and the professional character of teaching; "restructure the schools from bureaucracies to collegial organizations."

● Upgrade teacher salaries and working conditions. ECS presents career ladders that link advancement to evaluation of teaching practice and pay incentives for specific reasons as exemplary steps.

Principals

Principals should be instructional leaders and have the substantive knowledge and management skills needed for such leadership. They should:

● Establish a vision and strategic goals for the school and clear academic goals for student achievement, and direct the entire program toward these goals.

● Work out the following conditions in ways shown by research to promote effective teaching: use of time, class size and composition, grouping of students and teachers, curriculum coordination across grade levels and programs.

● Develop a climate of high expectations for student learning, collegial staff relationships focused on instruction, and public recognition of effective teachers.

● Work with staff in an open and collegial way; expect they know effective teaching research; participate and make presentations in staff development sessions; develop sanctions and rewards for teacher performance; buffer teachers from pressures.

School Organization

● Recognize individual schools as the main site for school improvement activities.

● Use existing school year and day to fullest for instruction by reducing administrative intrusions and time between class periods, and time for lunch, recess, and other nonacademic activities.

● Consider lengthening school year and day and extending teachers' contracts with extended time used for learning opportunities.

● "Launch an energetic program to reduce absenteeism [and]...community based programs to solve the dropout problem....efforts...include revitalizing course materials and making educational schedules flexible enough to accommodate students who have special problems."

School and Other Institutions and Resources

● District- or state-based consultants should work with administrators and teachers on a long-term basis.

● Business and labor leaders and scientific, engineering, and technical professionals must help schools by marshalling needed funds; communicating the skills needed in the work place; sharing expertise in planning, budgeting, and school management with school managers.

● Business leaders should work actively to establish partnerships with schools for activities such as team teaching, customized job training, job-site courses, and teacher awards.

● States and/or local boards should collaborate on enrichment programs for students and teachers.

* * * * *

Action for Excellence: A Comprehensive Plan to Improve Our Nation's Schools. Denver: Education Commission of the States, 1983. 52pp. $5.00

Brochures recommending actions that can be taken by various individuals and groups (principals, superintendents, local boards of education, legislators, governors, business, industry, and labor, chief state school officers, state boards of education, and college and university leaders) as well as a series of topical Issuegrams, are also available from the ECS as supplementary materials to Action for Excellence. In addition, ECS has published a list of over 180 statewide task forces now working on educational reform.

Education Commission of the States, 1860 Lincoln Street, Suite 300, Denver, CO 80295

PRINCETON: A PLACE FOR LEARNING, a report of the Long-Range Plan Advisory Committee to the Board of Education, Princeton Regional Schools, June 1983. Early in 1982 the Board of Education of the Princeton Regional Schools formed a long-range planning committee and charged it to develop "clear concepts of the world of tomorrow and the skills which will be needed to survive and flourish in that world." The committee was also to examine financing for the next decade, taking into account the decline in funds that would result from the shrinking student population. The committee was made up of 15 citizens who met frequently for a year and were aided by the consultation of community educators and other professionals.

Because the task of planning education for the problems of a changing society and the reality of shrinking funds are common to many communities, excerpts from this report are included as examples of the way one community thought about these problems. In 1980, Princeton Borough Township had a population of 25,718.

What Should Be Taught

● General Goals: "Functional literacy in the world entails four overriding education objectives: learning to think, to communicate, to cooperate, and to make decisions. Each objective carries with it the sense of control that empowers a person: control over self, confidence in interpersonal relations, competence in relations with the larger society."

● Mathematics: "The question of what constitutes mathematical literacy seems itself in flux. For example, while the ubiquitous electronic calculator has rendered many skills of written arithmetic all but obsolescent, it has also demanded new skills in the adaptation of computational algorithms to specific problems. Similarly, the vast amounts of data processed by computers have put new stress on the ability to judge the reasonableness of conclusions reached by means of those data.

"Our varied experience leads us to share the convictions of the National Council of Teachers of Mathematics that the skills considered basic must extend beyond computational facility to include: problem-solving; application of mathematics to everyday situations; approximation to orders of magnitude; interpretation and construction of tables, charts, and graphs; use of mathematics to predict; and computer literacy. Especially important among

84

these, we think, are the emphasis on problem-solving and the inclusion of probability and statistical inference. The effective use of mathematics rests on the ability to analyze problems and to devise strategies for their solution, while the pervasiveness of statistical data places a premium on knowing how to organize and interpret quantitative information and how to recognize the limits of quantification of a problem."

- <u>Science</u>: "The technological applications of scientific knowledge should figure prominently in the science curriculum, especially in the lower grades where all children must study the subject. In an era in which technological achievement and growth depend on scientific knowledge, and conversely, it seems strange, to say the least, that one still hears students asking of the science they are being taught, `But what use is it?'"

- <u>Language and Communication</u>: "[It is] essential that students gain experience as writers, speakers, readers, and listeners over the full range of genres....

"At issue is not fussiness over grammar and syntax, but rather inculcating in our children an appreciation of language as a means of thought in both senses of the term. It is a vehicle for expressing thought and a tool for shaping it....

"...dealing with complex technology based on abstract knowledge will require the ability to convey and to follow precise descriptions and instructions. Although modern telecommunication puts new emphasis on speaking and listening, it by no means entails the obsolescence of writing and reading.

"Perhaps even more important in a world increasingly inundated by the media of communication—TV, film, radio, even books—will be the skills of critical viewing, listening, and reading. Appreciating the artistry of the poet goes hand in hand with understanding the persuasiveness of the ad writer and deciphering the rhetoric of the politician."

- <u>Social Studies, Citizenship, History</u>: "The challenges of a pluralist society are likely to be best met by those who, appreciative of alternative ways of thinking and of differing systems of values, can comprehend what another person is saying in that person's terms.

"Many of the choices our children will have to make will be inherently uncertain. They will be better prepared to make them if their education has shown them that not all questions have a single "right" answer. By the same token, even in the face of uncertainty their decisions should be informed and well reasoned. They should know that for a given question some answers are in fact wrong.

"...things every citizen should know about our society [are]: the nature of representative democratic government; the mechanisms of local governance; the resolution of conflict through the rule of law and the procedures of the legal system; the structure of a modern economy with its systems of banking, investment, credit, and money; what the individual citizen may expect from society by way of rights; what society may expect from the individual citizen by way of responsibilities.

"...the history of technology taught as an integrated part of the history curriculum has its own important contribution to make to technological literacy. Similarly, having some understanding of the managerial structure of much technological research will be essential to intelligent discussion of the responsiveness of technology to social demands."

● The Arts: "The themes we have been expounding, especially awareness of others and the demands of modern society, only reinforce the importance of this area of the curriculum.

"First, not all communication is verbal. Humans also 'speak' to one another in signs and symbols, in rituals and gestures, in tones and pitches. The arts constitute a primary means of understanding and appreciating symbolic forms of communication, by which we often express the thoughts that elude language.

"Second, society in the next decades will depend heavily on innovation in the technological, economic, government-al, and social sectors. Americans will need a full measure of creative problem-solving. Current investigation into the properties of the right and left side of the brain provides evidence that the patterns of associative, analogical, divergent thinking characteristic of such innovation are in large part tactile and visual rather than verbal. Our access to them in education lies for the most part in the arts, which thus constitute a main element in the development of the whole mind.

Methods

"...beyond the basic disciplines, what subjects are taught is less important than how they are taught and the ends to which they are taught. There are many ways of exploring heritage, as there are various approaches to uncovering the workings of society or of scouting the domain of experience and learning. When an educational program is guided by a concept of functional literacy, integration rather than coverage becomes the measure of comprehensiveness."

School Organization

"Many current courses and methods, and some of the existing structure of departments and specialties (particularly at the secondary level), are unlikely to survive the combined pressures of shrinking enrollments, interdisciplinary approaches, and new instructional objectives."

Teachers

"For some staff members [new interdisciplinary assignments] may involve additional study in subject areas (e.g., computers) and in teaching methods (to enhance, for example, the heuristic give-and-take of the classroom and to encourage interactive and questioning attitudes among students). We do not assume, however, that any particular kind of training or experiences will provide the answer. A wide range of devices might have a place in the total scheme, from individual graduate study to in-house seminars or to service on interdisciplinary task forces charged with developing specific curricula and provided with released time from teaching duties and budgetary support for outside consultants....

"Without meaning to suggest what particular devices might be used, we wish to incorporate a simple estimate based on the equivalent of one sabbatical term every seven years....the active involvement and professional development of the faculty will be one of the most crucial factors in bringing about a successful transition to the educational programs of the future, and one where short-sighted economics should be avoided....

"...We should...maintain a salary scale as much as 5% higher than that of comparable districts in the state. Asking for more from our teachers, we should offer them more for their services."

Administration

"The professional development of the administration may, in some ways, be as important as that of the teaching faculty, for the more highly focused goals and tightly defined curriculum will require managerial expertise of a special order....

"...It has seemed reasonable to allow an `administrative contingency´ to be used for higher salaries, cost of training, or equivalent investments in management resources. In the word `equivalent´ we are recognizing, as in the case of the teaching staff, that no standard program exists for inculcating the knowledge and skills for administrative leadership in the task at hand."

* * * * *

Long-Range Plan Advisory Committee to the Board of Education. Princeton: A Place for Learning. Princeton, N.J.: Princeton Regional Schools, 1983. 70 pp.

Dr. Paul D. Houston, Superintendent, Princeton Regional Schools, Box 711, Princeton, NJ 08540

EDUCATING AMERICANS FOR THE 21st CENTURY: A Plan of Action for Improving Mathematics, Science and Technology Education for All American Elementary and Secondary Students So That Their Achievement Is the Best in the

World by 1995, issued in 1983 by the National Science Board Commission on Precollege Education in Mathematics, Science and Technology.

The two-volume report is based on the premise that the declining quality of science, mathematics, and technology education harms this country's productive capacity, its standard of living, and its standing as a world power. It offers a comprehensive plan to improve math, science, and technology education; many generative examples of ways schools already carry out two of the recommendations (enhancing teacher compensation and using computers for instruction); and rationales and outlines for curricular revision. We have focused on the recommendations for high schools, but the report deals with the full K-12 continuum.

What Should Be Taught

All secondary school students should be required to take at least three years of mathematics and of science and technology, including one year of algebra and one semester of computer science. All secondary schools should offer advanced mathematics and science courses. This requirement should be in place by September 1, 1985.

The curriculum must be rethought, updated, and reorganized, bringing in the areas of technology and engineering, and important new emphases and topics. The following recommendations that deal with curriculum revision are drawn from both the main report and from working committee reports, and, therefore, not all may have the backing of the full commission.

• Mathematics: "At the secondary level there is a need to examine the content, emphasis, and approaches of courses in algebra, geometry, precalculus methods and trigonometry. Some components in the traditional school mathematics curriculum have little importance in the light of new technologies. The current sequence, which isolates geometry in a year-long course rather than integrating aspects of geometry over several years with other mathematics courses, must be seriously challenged. Some concepts of geometry are needed by all students.

Other components can be streamlined, leaving room for important new topics.
- Discrete mathematics, elementary statistics and probability should now be considered fundamental for all high school students.

"The development of computer science as well as computer technology suggests new approaches to the teaching of all mathematics in which emphasis should be on:
- Algorithmic thinking as an essential part of problem-solving.
- Student data-gathering and exploration of mathematical ideas in order to facilitate learning mathematics by discovery."

● Science: "The desired outcomes of science instruction involve understanding and appreciation of the external and internal biological and physical environments. Such learning must clearly be a lifelong process...."

"The number of topics covered in high school science courses should be drastically reduced. Attention should then be directed toward the integration of remaining facts, concepts and principles within each discipline and with other sciences and areas such as mathematics, technology and the social sciences. Ideas should be selected which can be developed honestly at a level comprehensible to high school students; developed out of experimental evidence that high school students can gather or, at least, understand; and tie into other parts of the course so that their use can be reinforced by practice. In addition, all courses should provide opportunities to develop the ability to read science materials.

Biology: "The teaching emphasis at all grade levels is largely upon learning the names of plants and animals, their structural parts and the function of each. The student complaint is that "there are too many names and terms to learn....

"The primary need for the revitalization of biology education is perceived to be a conceptual framework that is more in harmony with understanding oneself and which is supportive of the national and global welfare....

"General biology in the high school (grade 10) should emphasize biological knowledge in a social/ecological context....The advanced or second level course in high school biology should be taught in the context of a discipline emphasizing its structure, its modes of inquiry, its theoretical underpinnings, and its career opportunities.

"All students would be expected to enroll in the biological offerings in the elementary and middle/junior high schools and in the general biology course of the senior high school."

Chemistry: "At all levels, the social and human relevance of chemistry should be emphasized.   Problem-solving skills and application of scientific processes should be continually developed.   Instruction should incorporate a proper selection and integration of topics from both descriptive chemistry and theoretical chemistry."

Physics: "Precollege physics should be taught so as to demonstrate the general principles of seeking and knowing in science.   The relevance of the understanding which physics provides to present and future problems and opportunities of our civilization should be constantly demonstrated and emphasized."

● Technology and Engineering: "The emergence of high technology in the past generation has added another dimension of knowledge needed for dealing with world affairs.   It is just as important for the young student to be able to understand and appreciate what science and technology are and what they can and cannot do for society as it has been to study the other areas which society has come to regard as essential in the education of young people.   Scientific and technological literacy is needed to understand many of the issues, including those on local, national, and international levels, on which our citzens will vote or express their opinions in other ways....

"This need does not call for the addition of special new courses.   Rather, it calls for a careful incorporation of the concepts of mathematics and science and their prac-

91

tical application into courses presently available in many subjects, particularly courses such as social sciences and history. Even mathematics instruction can be made more interesting and useful by incorporating various scientific and technological concepts within the course presentations.

"Technological literacy is the possession of a reasonable understanding of the behavior of technological systems and requires knowledge of scientific and mathematical concepts. Along with this must go an understanding of certain underlying concepts that are unique to engineering."

To illustrate the content of technology education, the report lists the following technological systems as ones to be studied:
Communications; energy production and conservation; transportation; shelter; food production; health care delivery; safety; residential use of space; resource management; biotechnology; computers and their applications; and nuclear issues.

And the following concepts:
Problem formulation and solving; debugging a problem; discovering alternative solutions to problems; making connections between theory and practice; pattern recognition; engineering approaches to problems-- evaluating trade-offs; probability/approximation/ examination; building and testing of equipment; examining trade-offs and risk analysis; economic decision making; feedback and stability; and recognizing orders of magnitude.

The report gives examples of how such systems and concepts can be integrated into other subject areas.

Methods

● "There should be a de-emphasis on lectures in favor of activities in problem solving, modeling, estimating, probability, and statistics."

● "The study of technology should be used as a way of unifying the teaching of science at the secondary level."

Media

This report gives a vision of the potential of audio-
visual and computer technology, qualified with specific
and general caveats:

● Development: "Modern computer technology clearly has
vast potential for enriching and enlivening the secondary
school curriculum. However,...there is need for research
on the effects of incorporating technology into the
traditional secondary school curriculum. We urge federal
support for investigations into this question, including
development of experimental materials and prototypes of
actual school curricula."

● General Use: "Television and other audio-visual technologies can be used to stimulate thought, activities,
and problem solving, and to graphically illustrate worlds
of place, size, and complexity otherwise difficult to
access. Calculators and computers can provide the computational and modeling power necessary for solving problems of real interest and can develop new systematic
thought processes....It is realized, however, that great
care must be taken to avoid the overuse and misuse of
communication and computation technologies in education
that may arise because of the fascination of the media
and our lack of experience about their effects....these
tools [should] not be used to replace the self-checking
learning that comes from interaction with reality, nor to
replace the teacher in the bulk of situations where the
teacher's understanding of student response is important.
Television programs and computer software need to be
developed specifically for the recommended curriculum."

● For Mathematics: "New computer technology allows not
only the introduction of pertinent new material into the
curriculum and new ways to teach traditional mathematics,
but it also casts doubt on the importance of some of the
traditional curriculum. Particularly noteworthy in this
context at the secondary level are:
- Symbolic manipulation systems which...will allow
students to do symbolic algebra at a far more sophisticated level than they can be expected to do with pencil
and paper.
- Computer graphics and the coming interactive video-

disc system which will enable the presentation and manipulation of geometric and numerical objects...to enhance the presentation of much secondary school mathematical material.

"We stress that the use of this technology and related software packages is not a substitute for the understanding of the essential elements of mathematics, but rather is a means to enhance understanding and stimulate creativity."

● For Physics: "We welcome the use of computers in the physics classroom and laboratory if they are (1) used to increase the sophistication and satisfaction of problem solving; (2) taken advantage of in the laboratory for real time data collection, display, analysis, and storage; and/or (3) used to simulate real world situations that cannot easily be observed through direct demonstrations, laboratory experiments or field trips.

"We are not excited about the use of computers as an expensive set of 'flash cards' and believe that the replacement of direct labs or demonstration experiences by computer simulations is inconsistent with the evidence on how people learn from concrete real world experiences."

● A General Caution: "The disparity of access between children who have a computer at home and children who do not, threatens to widen the educational gap that already exists between different economic strata. It is urgent that programs be designed to address this problem."

Teachers

● Both elementary and secondary teachers should be computer literate. Teacher training should incorporate the use of calculators and computers in mathematics and science instruction.

● Secondary school mathematics and science teachers should have a full major in college mathematics and science, a limited number of effective education courses, and practice teaching under a qualified teacher.

94

• Top priority must be placed on obtaining, retraining, and retaining teachers of high quality in mathematics, science, and technology, and providing them with a work environment in which they can be effective.

• State and local governments should work to improve the teaching environment. This includes greater administrative and parental support of discipline and attendance, fewer classroom interruptions, and higher academic standards, as well as the provision of needed equipment, materials, and specialized support staff.

• School systems should explore means to adjust compensation in order to compete for and retain high quality teachers in fields like mathematics, science, and technology. Compensation calculations must include consideration of intangible benefits such as the length of the work year, promotion potential, and similar factors.

• State and local governments should provide means for teachers to move up a salary and status ladder without leaving the classroom.

• Local school systems, military and other governmental entities, and the private sector should all explore ways to extend the employment year while providing supplementary income and revitalizing experience.

• Every state should establish at least one regional training and resource center where teachers can obtain supporting services such as computer instruction and software and curriculum evaluation.

• State and local school systems should draw upon the staffs of industry, universities, the military and other government departments, and retired scientists to provide sources of qualified teaching assistance. Local systems should take actions to facilitate the entry and classroom training of such special teachers.

School Organization

• Considerably more time should be devoted to mathematics, science, and technology throughout the elementary and secondary grades. This will require that the school day, week, and/or year be substantially lengthened.

● The practice of social promotion should be curtailed.

Schools and Other Institutions

● Each school district should carry out programs to eliminate barriers that discriminate against students on the basis of race, gender, ethnic background, or socio-economic status.

● School districts and community colleges should cooperate in assisting students whose preparation is inadequate to allow them to take the next steps in their education.

● Every state should establish rigorous standards for high school graduation, and local school districts should provide rigorous standards for grade promotion.

● Colleges and universities should phase in higher mathematics and science entrance requirements, including four years of high school mathematics (including a second year of algebra), course work covering probability and statistics, four years of high school science (including physics and chemistry), and one semester of computer science.

● Local school boards should foster partnerships with business, government, and academia to encourage, aid, and support in solving the academic and financial problems of their schools.

● Youth organizations, museums, broadcasters, and other agents of informal education should endeavor to make the environment for informal learning as rich as possible.

● Local business groups and organizations with related interests should work with museums to supplement and encourage their activities and to create new programs that let children see science and technology in the real world.

● The federal government should encourage and finance, in part, the establishment of exemplary programs in mathematics, science, and technology in every community which would serve as examples and catalysts for upgrading all schools.

● State governments should promote and local school districts should establish such programs as a major strategy toward upgrading all schools.

* * * * *

Today's Problems, Tomorrow's Crises: A Report of the National Science Board Commission on Precollege Education in Mathematics, Science and Technology. Washington, D.C.: National Science Board/National Science Foundation, 1982. 8 pp.

Educating Americans for the 21st Century: A Plan of Action for Improving Mathematics, Science and Technology Education for all American Elementary and Secondary Students So That Their Achievement Is the Best in the World by 1995: A Report to the American People and the National Science Board. Washington, D.C.: National Science Board Commission on Precollege Education in Mathematics, Science and Technology, 1983. 124 pp.

A volume of Source Materials (251 pages) accompanies the above publication.

The National Science Board Commission on Precollege Education, National Science Foundation, Room 420, Washington D.C. 20550

HIGH SCHOOL: A REPORT ON SECONDARY EDUCATION IN AMERICA, a study directed by Ernest L. Boyer, former U.S. Commissioner of Education, for the Carnegie Foundation for the Advancement of Teaching. The project involved two years of literature review and intensive ethnographic study in 15 high schools. The purposes of the study are to present a profile of American high schools today and a comprehensive set of recommendations for secondary education.

Boyer emphasizes the importance for a school of a clear, shared vision of its goals, and he focuses on:

- Mastery of language for communication.

- Development of the capacity to think critically.

- Learning about oneself, the human heritage, and the interdependent world through a core curriculum based on important human experience and ideas.

- Preparation for work and further education through electives that develop individual aptitudes and interests.

- School and community service.

What Should Be Taught

- Mastery of the English Language

English Language Proficiency: To be assessed for each student the year before high school, and a pre-high-school summer program provided for remedial work, directed at each student's difficulties. For those who continue to need help, an intensive program in the initial term with help available thereafter.

Basic English: A course with emphasis on writing, in which teachers have time to evaluate and respond to what students write. Classes should have no more than twenty students, and no teacher should have more than two such classes.

The Spoken Word: Speaking and listening to be included as a subject of study in order to improve communication.

- The Core Curriculum: Boyer proposes a core curriculum to comprise for all students two-thirds of the credits needed for graduation. It consists of a study of those consequential ideas, experiences, and traditions common to all of us by virtue of our membership in the human family at a particular moment in history. The content of the core curriculum must extend beyond specialties and focus on more transcendent issues.

Literature: One year to introduce students to the power of the written word as "both mirror and the lamp of

98

time"--from Greek playwrights to modern authors; basic human questions, motivations, and dilemmas.

United States History: A one-year study of people, issues, and ideas that have shaped our national heritage, using primary sources--autobiographies, diaries, letters.

Western Civilization: One year tracing development of human communities from tribes to city-states to nations, and the evolution of our cultural, political, religious, and moral ideas. Explore historical moments of both high achievement and degradation.

Non-Western Civilization: One semester to convey the richness and connectedness of human experience and outside perspectives on our own culture, approached through studying the development of one non-Western nation.

Civics: One year on the traditions of democratic thought and workings of American government, approached through individual study of a currently contested issue.

Science and the Natural World: A two-year sequence including basic courses in biological and physical sciences, taught for understanding of general principles and processes of science.

Mathematics: A two-year sequence to develop the ability to use math to solve problems, emphasizing identifying problems, structuring solutions, testing reasonableness of solutions.

Technology: One semester on the history of tools, the ethical and social issues raised by technology. Where and why computers should be used is more important than "hands-on" computer experience.

Foreign Language: Some proficiency with the language of another culture, with a foundation in elementary schools and at least two years of the language in high school; Spanish should be offered because of our Hispanic population and neighbors.

The Arts: An opportunity to study how human beings communicate not only with words but through music, dance, and the visual arts, and how the arts are the means by which a culture can be measured.

Health: Knowledge about health is crucial. Students should learn about the human body in all stages of the life cycle and how physical health contributes to emotional well-being; the teacher must have specialized in health education.

Work: One semester on the meaning of vocation that explores the historical, social, and economic aspects of work, attitude changes through the years, and differences from one culture to another; what determines the status and rewards of different work; the changing market for different jobs. An in-depth study of one specific occupation.

Independent Study: As a senior project to encourage interdisciplinary thinking, a written report on a contemporary issue that draws upon the academic fields studied. For one-half credit; each teacher responsible for a small number of students.

• Transition to Work and Further Study: The first two years of high school would be devoted almost exclusively to the common core, and some of this work would continue into the third or fourth year. The last two years should be a transition program in which about half the time is devoted to "elective clusters."

Elective clusters should be a carefully designed program that includes advanced study in selected academic subjects, the exploration of career options, or a combination of both. Examples of clusters: health services, the arts, computers. In order to offer a full range of elective clusters, high schools must establish connections with institutions beyond the schools—such as libraries, museums, art galleries, colleges, and industrial laboratories.

• Service: The New Carnegie Unit: A new "Carnegie unit" for opportunity to feel responsibly engaged with others, a service requirement of volunteer work in community or school; weekly meetings to review experiences, discuss problems.

Methods

● <u>Active Class Participation</u>: A variety of teaching styles—lecturing to transmit information, coaching to teach a skill, and Socratic questioning to enlarge understanding. But there should be a particular emphasis on the active participation of the student.

● <u>Interdisciplinary Approach</u>: Current instruction is compartmentalized and gives a narrow view of both knowledge and reality. Interdisciplinary approaches should touch larger issues. Teachers must make the connections between disciplines.

● <u>Individualization</u>: The teaching of writing, as proposed in the curriculum, requires more one-to-one teaching time; many of the proposed improvements require small groups rather than large classes.

● <u>Time Pressure</u>: Science, foreign language, and in-depth explorations in other areas call for a sense that time is flexible and at the service of learning rather than rigidly defined by the bell.

● <u>Depth vs. Coverage</u>: Examples throughout the proposed curriculum suggest that what is important is not coverage but depth and meaningful material: in history the approach proposed is studying the development of a community, or lives of people who have shaped our history; in civics it is studying the evolution of a contested issues; in math it is focusing on learning how to identify and solve problems on one's own; in science it is focusing on scientific principles and method.

Materials and Media

● "Most textbooks present...a highly simplified view of reality and practically no insight into the methods by which the information has been gathered....[they] seldom communicate...the richness and excitement of original works...." Teachers should use more original sources instead of relying so heavily on textbooks.

● States should ease control over textbook selection, and the district and local school system should, instead, have the authority, with teachers having a greater voice in their subject areas.

● Technology, from television to computers, can help teachers to individualize instruction.

● Schools should not buy computers or other expensive equipment until they are very clear about why, how, and when it is to be used.

● In purchasing computers, schools should consider the quality of the instructional material available and the commitment of the computer company to developing instructional materials for the school.

● Computer firms selling to schools should consult with teachers in developing software and help provide up-to-date information and training in computer use.

● In each community, one cable channel should be re-served for schools to provide inservice programs for teachers, homework help for students, and outstanding arts and sciences programming.

Teachers

Boyer proposes the following improvements:

● Recruitment starting in high school with "cadet teachers" and continuing in college with scholarships for the top 5% who enter teaching programs.

● No more than four daily formal class meetings and one period for small seminars and independent projects; 60 minutes reserved for preparation.

● No monitoring halls and lunch rooms; this should be done by clerical staff and parent and student volunteers.

● More autonomy in choice of teaching materials and ways of evaluating student work.

● Better working conditions, including adequate supplies, permanent working space, pleasant place for breaks and lunch, and effective protection from violence.

● Improved intellectual climate, with encouragement of collegial interaction over professional issues and the school becoming a "center of inquiry" about teaching; a Teacher Excellence Fund in every school to provide competitive grants for teachers to develop special projects.

● A two-week paid Professional Development Term added to the school year for study and instruction improvement, to be planned mainly by teachers at the district level.

● Sabbaticals, study leaves, or exchanges with other school systems for renewal and gaining perspective. Every five years teachers with a study plan should be eligible for a paid Summer Study Term; a Teacher Travel Fund should exist to cover conference travel.

● Salary averages increased by 25% beyond inflation over the next three years, with immediate entry-level increases; raises should come with career advancement; there should be no differential scales for different disciplines.

● A career ladder in which top rungs do not represent leaving teaching. The steps should be: credentialing by board of senior classroom teachers, associate teacher working two years under mentorship and direct supervision; full teacher status for three years with assessment by master teacher panel; senior teacher status for some, who would be mentors to associate teachers.

● More recognition and rewards, such as public and parental demonstration of support, honorary degrees from local colleges, cash awards from government and business.

● In fields with teacher shortages, programs to permit qualified professionals to teach part-time--for example, recently retired college professors, business and industry personnel.

Principals

Recommended are the following proposals:

● The same preparation as teachers, because principals cannot lead without classroom experience, followed by:

103

two years as "associate teacher"; a program to develop skills in decision making, organization, and planning, written and oral communication; a year as "administrative intern"; two years as "assistant principal."

● More control over school budgets with authority to allocate funds within guidelines set by district office.

● A Discretionary School Fund for special programs.

● Responsibility over the selection of teachers and leeway to reward good teachers.

● A network of Academies for Principals for continuing education, updating on developments in education.

● Special recognition for outstanding principals through, for example, days freed for site visits, meetings with colleagues, university study.

Guidance and Evaluation

● Guidance services must be expanded so that no counselor has more than one hundred students, and a community agency referral service should be available.

● A Student Achievement and Advisement Test (SAAT) should be developed to assess what all students have learned and advise about their futures. It should include achievement tests, teacher evaluations, and student portfolios of academic and vocational work samples.

● Every high school should periodically survey graduates to assess long-range performance.

School Organization

● The current three-track system (academic, vocational, general) should be abolished and replaced by a single track providing a common core for all students.

● Required courses should make up two-thirds of the units required for high school graduation.

• "Lengthening the school year is not a top priority for school reform. The urgent need is not more time but better use of time."

• A more flexible class schedule should be worked out to allow longer blocks of time, especially for laboratory science, foreign language, creative writing, and to permit greater depth. Students can save time traveling between classes and gain, for example, the opportunity both to write and have writing evaluated in same period.

• Classes, such as basic English, should be limited in size to allow individual attention to student writing.

• Schools with more than 1500 students should consider reorganizing into smaller units of several hundred.

Special Student Populations

• Options for gifted students to work at their own pace should be provided, such as independent study with a mentor; permission to "test-out" of a course to a more advanced one or to a course at nearby colleges; the International Baccalaureate program.

• To prevent high-risk students from dropping out, patterns of school failure should be identified early and treated remedially. Alternative schools should be set up to give intensive, continuous help, with a sense of belonging and structure. "At the heart of every effort that appeared to be succeeding...there was a close relationship between a student and a counselor or teacher... with high standards...one who had gained the student's... trust."

• High school districts should work with community colleges to create a reentry arrangement that allows dropouts to complete education.

The School Plant

• The condition of many school buildings is an emergency that calls for a federal response. A federal program should be set up to help schools improve school plants and buy equipment."

105

Schools and Other Institutions

Boyer makes many thoughtful recommendations for supportive action on the part of school boards, colleges, businesses, and state and federal agencies. Because we view the proposed core curriculum as a unique contribution to the general pool of recommendations, we have chosen to devote available space to that and to refer readers interested in the role of other institutions to the book.

* * * * *

Boyer, Ernest L. <u>High School: A Report on Secondary Education in America</u>. New York: Harper & Row, 1983. 363 pp. $15.00

A PLACE CALLED SCHOOL: PROSPECTS FOR THE FUTURE, by John I. Goodlad, former dean of the Graduate School of Education at UCLA. The book reports on an eight-year in-depth study of 38 schools examined in triples. The study was conducted under the auspices of the Institute for Development of Educational Activities, Inc., an affiliate of the Charles F. Kettering Foundation, and was financed by 14 agencies.

Goodlad's research project, "A Study of Schooling," used observations of 1,016 high school classrooms and interviews and questionnaires, to study schooling from the perspective of a full range of the participants in the education process. The study compares their beliefs about what constitutes good education with the reality of what goes on in classrooms; examines how our current way of schooling fits current social conditions and needs; and explores ways to design schooling for results that are closer to ideals and more appropriate for our times. The observation team was particularly struck by student passivity in classrooms, and many of the recommendations are made with this problem in mind.

Goodlad presents a list of goals derived from both historical review and an analysis of recent state documents. From his research he concluded that schools have always been expected to provide more than the "three

106

R's" and that the following list does not represent only current expectations. Goodlad's list is fully detailed, including specific abilities, knowledge, and understandings. Because it is too long to include here, we present the general categories and refer interested readers to the book:

● <u>Academic</u>, embracing all intellectual skills and domains of knowledge.

● <u>Vocational</u>, geared to developing readiness for productive work and economic responsibility.

● <u>Social and civic</u>, related to preparing for socialization into a complex society.

● <u>Personal</u>, emphasizing the development of individual responsibility, talent, and free expression.

What Should Be Taught

● The curriculum should provide "a common core of studies from which students cannot escape through electives"; eliminate tracking, which leads to differences in subject matter, expectations, and teacher treatment.

● Central principles should be sorted out from the "clutter of specifics....A few concepts should be learned through a variety of approaches."

● The "five fingers of human knowledge and organized experience" should be accorded percentages of a student's program, as follows:
- Mathematics and science: up to 18%.
- Language and literature: up to 18%.
- Society and social studies: up to 15%.
- The arts: up to 15%.
- The vocations: up to 15%.

Physical education should be accorded 10%, and 10% left for courses that would develop individual interests and talents. Within each of the five domains, two-thirds of all students' programs should be common, the rest selected from a limited set of electives. This plan would result in a common "core curriculum."

● What should be common about the core is not a set of topics, but a set of concepts, principles, skills, and ways of knowing.

● The sixth domain—individual choice—allows a student to develop and refine an individual interest or talent and "may be the most significant...in determining life-long commitments and accomplishments." It can be pursued by in-school or out-of-school offerings, and vouchers are recommended. This domain must never be taken over for remedial purposes.

● Remedial work must be accomplished within the maximum time allowed for a domain; the one-third not in common in each domain can be used for remedial or advanced work.

● "The vocations" does not mean training for specific jobs, but would include rather "a measure of technological literacy—especially in computers—and awareness of how economics function, some understanding of economic principles such as cost effectiveness, and a broad exposure to careers and work." Visits to business and industry would be accompanied by extensive reading, writing, and discussion.

● Critical abilities—termed "technological literacy"—should be developed that can be applied to newspapers, advertising, and all forms of television. Teaching computer literacy is also a responsibility of the schools.

Methods

Goodlad describes patterns of teaching observed with surprising regularity in over 1000 classrooms:

> ...The domination of the teacher is obvious in the conduct of instruction. Most of the time the teacher is engaged in either frontal teaching, monitoring students' seat-work, or conducting quizzes. Relatively rarely are students actively engaged in learning directly from one another or in initiating processes of interaction with teachers. When students work in smaller groups, they usually are doing the same things side by side, and these things tend to be determined by the teacher.

There is a paucity of praise and correction of students' performance, as well as of teacher guidance in how to do better next time. Teachers tend not to respond in overtly positive or negative ways to the work students do.

Students generally engage in a rather narrow range of classroom activities—listening to teachers, writing answers to questions, and taking tests and quizzes. Strikingly similar "schooling activities" transcend teachers, grade levels, and subjects. Students receive relatively little exposure to audio-visual aids, field trips, or guest lecturers. Except in [such "nonacademic" subjects as] the arts, physical education, and vocational education, there is little hands-on activity. Acting out, role playing, dance, the manipulation of materials, and the like are rarely used....[Ironically, these are the types of activities students like most, and they could be used to advantage to provide variety in academic areas.]

...there was strong evidence of students not having time to finish their lessons or not understanding what the teacher wanted them to do. A significant percentage saw themselves as not getting sufficient teacher help with mistakes and difficulties. (pp. 123-24)

Goodlad offers the following observations toward improving teaching methods:

● "No single variable in itself appears sufficiently powerful to influence student learning significantly. Rather it appears that each of a number of approaches carries some weight, and orchestrated together, they can add up to a significant difference."

● One approach is "arranging and rearranging instructional groups and methods to achieve changing purposes—for example, shifting from large group instruction involving lecturing to small groups necessitating student interaction."

● Another is "varying the focus of learning from textbooks to films, to field trips, to library research in order to assure different avenues to the same learnings."

• Another approach stresses clear instructions, support, and feedback; good performance is praised; errors or faulty approaches are pointed out quickly; a learner having unusual trouble with a particular method is given an alternative to the one used by the total group; diagnostic quizzes used for "self-appraisal and corrective action... before an exam 'that counts' is given."

• "It is encouraging that what is associated with students' satisfaction frequently is found also to be associated with students' performance. And, finally, it is encouraging that many teachers believe these procedures to be desirable, whether or not they practice them."

• "Factors thought to be negatively associated with learning tend to be a reverse of the above. To be avoided is the daily repetition of classroom activities that encourage passivity and rote behavior on the part of students--pedagogy that is not sensitively responsive to what is happening to individuals. Some students thrive no matter what the instructor's approach, but also we know that students appearing to be less able can and do approach the learning levels of those successful students when instruction is dovetailed to their special needs."

• "For most students academic learning is too abstract. They need to see, touch, and smell what they read and write about. Time spent visiting a newspaper press, examining artifacts, or observing a craftsman provides reality and stimulus for later reading, explaining, and discussing. Drawing or building can be an alternative way of gaining insight."

• Effective teaching in social studies and science calls for visits to governmental bodies in session, fields and ponds, industrial laboratories....Teaching such subjects well calls for departing from methods and workbooks in seeking to use multiple resources--films, an array of source books, perhaps construction materials, and small conference rooms."

Guidance

• "Schools need (1) data to pinpoint those students... least able to help themselves, and (2)...practices de-

110

signed to assist (them)...in becoming confident and resourceful." Some students are involved in almost everything--those who do well academically also tend to participate in extracurricular activities that heighten and positive feelings about school; schools need to reach the students who don't participate.

Teachers

● Preservice and inservice training should focus on:

- "The process of humanizing knowledge," which involves both the teachers' enthusiasm for a subject and pedagogical techniques to keep the student interested.

- Opportunities to see and use techniques to elicit problem solving, imaginative essays, grasp of complex phenomena such as functions of our government compared with others, and techniques such as varying teaching methods, providing students with knowledge of their performance, giving praise for good work. Video taping can help self-examination and improvement.

● Teachers should be employed for an additional month per year, time which would be devoted to planning the local school program.

● Teaching hours should be reduced to provide more time for planning, working with individual students, reading student papers.

● Teachers should have a say in how money allocated to their school is spent--for example, in requesting "six copies of each of five books rather than 30 copies of a single book."

● They should have the time and opportunity to work together on school-based issues. District budgets should allow for 180 days of teaching and 20 days of planning time.

● They should have a career ladder starting with assisting and apprentice roles, with salary differentiation corresponding to differentiation in function and preparation.

111

● A head teacher should be employed at each school, chosen in a nationwide search for candidates who are highly successful teachers and have a clinical doctorate; the head teacher would teach part-time, be a role model, monitor all teaching, and provide inservice assistance such as diagnosis of difficult learning problems.

Principals

● In contrast to a head teacher, the principal's role should be to create the school conditions conducive to learning—a full-time job in itself.

● Principals should have the resource of a policy and planning group—chaired by the principal and including teachers, students, parents, a representative from the district office. Such a group working to identify problems, gather data, formulate solutions is essential in giving a school self-renewing capacity.

● Each district should identify a pool of potential principal candidates and cultivate a pool so it has candidates available when a principalship is vacated. The pool might extend well beyond district lines.

School, District, and State

● States should not focus on principals and individual schools for accountability, but should hold districts accountable for communicating state goals, developing balanced curricula, providing time and resources for local school improvement, assuring equity in distribution of resources. Schools, in turn, should have the authority to develop long-term staffing plans, and their own budgets. Schools should be semiautonomous but have the support of the district and the network of other schools.

School Organization

● Age: Ideally, school should begin at age 4 and end with a completion certificate at age 16. Costs would be less because public kindergarten will be included in the span, and, at the upper end, costs in developing curriculum, teacher frustration, policing schools, and monitoring vandalism will be reduced. In current circum-

112

stances where students leave at 18, a marked swing in school focus toward the world of work might be appropriate at 16.

● School Year: Time spent in school appears to affect directly amount learned, especially in math, science, and literature. Increasing the school year from 175 to 185 days appears to enhance achievement. Therefore days for purposes such as inservice education should not be taken out of the school year but added to it.

● Teacher Time: Instructional time should be reduced to 20 hours a week and the remaining time used for teacher development. It might be more effective to have only three to four hours daily of academics, and the rest of the time for nonacademic activities such as the development of talents with nonteaching adults supervising.

● Size: The most satisfying schools in the sample were the smallest; the least satisfying were the largest. Where schools are large a "house" structure can break them down into smaller units—each house should have its own curriculum, faculty, counselors, students; with house-to-house sharing of special facilities and activities. The house structure should last three or four years to assure long-term association with a group of students and teachers.

● Tracking: With several grade levels available in a house structure, students who are slower in a subject do not need to be tracked into inferior content. They simply need more time and support in seeking to reach mastery. The principles involved are those of continuous progress and nongrading. "Eliminate any arrangement that groups students in same subject into different classrooms based on past performance—i.e. tracking."

* * * * *

Goodlad, John I. A Place Called School: Prospects for the Future. New York: McGraw-Hill, 1984. 396 pp. $18.95

Further books based on the data collected for A Study of Schooling are currently being written. A list of technical reports issued by A Study of Schooling and

113

available through ERIC appears in Appendix A of <u>A Place Called School</u>.

<u>HORACE'S COMPROMISE; THE DILEMMA OF THE AMERICAN HIGH SCHOOL</u>, by Theodore R. Sizer, 1984. This book is the first of three volumes to result from "A Study of High Schools," a five-year study sponsored by the National Association of Secondary School Principals and the National Association of Independent Schools. Sizer and a staff of 20 researchers and field observers visited over 80 schools and did concentrated observations of daily life in 15--both public and private. The book attempts to share this experience with the reader, conveying the "feel" and complexity of life in American high schools.

Sizer believes that the purpose of secondary schooling is primarily to cultivate the qualities of mind needed for participation in American society, and his book focuses on the teacher as central to that process. "Horace" is an able and dedicated teacher who constantly has to compromise what he knows to be the best practice because of the multitude of demands on his time. Sizer explores the full range of conditions teachers have to work with--school climate, use of time and space, values, resources, curricula, student attitude, the administrative hierarchy--analyzing <u>what is</u> and asking what <u>should be</u> in order to enable teachers to work effectively. He concurs with and builds on many of the recommendations of the Paideia project.

"Less is more" is a principle Sizer applies throughout his recommendations, starting with general goals for compulsory education upon which more advanced high school studies are added:

● <u>Literacy</u>: "...the ability to comprehend and to understand ideas and arguments to a degree that allows an individual to use them"; the ability to "read easily and sensitively enough to comprehend at least the basic arguments presented by contemporary and social life."

● <u>Numeracy</u>: "...the ability both to use numbers arithmetically and algebraically and to understand the concepts, relationships, and logic embedded in mathematical thought."

• Civic understanding: "...a grasp of the basis for consensual democratic government, a respect for its processes, and acceptance of the restraints and obligations incumbent on a citizen.

"Although these three claims of the state are minimal, they should be maximal, as well. They provide the essential context for responsible citizenship and government. Since democracy could not long survive without them, it is reasonable for the state to insist on their mastery and to tax its citizens to ensure that each citizen has the means to gain their mastery. However, beyond these three elements, the claims of the state have far less merit. The state has no right to insist that I be `employable'...."

What Should Be Taught

In discussing content, Sizer makes three strong points:

• It is not the information that is important but rather learning how to use it. "The world around us, for good or ill, is a more insistent, rich, and effective provider of information than was our grandparents'. Education's job today is less in purveying information than in helping people to use it--that is, to exercise their minds."

• The particular subject matter chosen may differ with each situation. Choices should be made available. Two principles should be applied in selecting content: subject matter should support the learning of skills, and it "should lead somewhere, in the eyes...of the student...it must connect to wherever that student is rooted...and... promise to take him to an important place."

• "`Less is more.' I believe that the qualities of mind that should be the goal of high school need time to grow and that they develop best when engaging a few important ideas, deeply."

"The load of data purveyed in a typical high school year is staggering....If there is pressure...to cover ground, more time is spent informing and less on the process of individual knowing." In addition, fewer subjects greatly reduce scheduling problems and promote flexibility.

● Sizer gives as one example of curriculum a model that organizes study into four large areas:

Inquiry and Expression: Writing is most important, but all kinds of communication should be included--visual, gesture, nuance, tone, even typewriting and handwriting, as both are necessary for modern communication. "English" as such would disappear and its elements would be taught in several of these areas.

Mathematics and Science: Both are the language of "certainties"; merge these two traditional departments, perhaps using computer science as the "glue" between them.

Literature and the Arts: The varied "attempts to find meaning" should be studied together, the written, spoken, and nonverbal arts.

Philosophy and History: History is the most difficult subject for high school students because it is an abstraction of the past; the most engaging initial approach is autobiography--of either individuals or communities. Political, moral, ethical philosophy is a powerful subject for adolescents because it can build on their search for values.

● Other Areas:

Electives can be accommodated within these broad areas. Sizer has recommendations for other areas included in current schooling, as follows:

Physical education belongs in school and should be taught in the science-math area.

Vocational education should not be provided at the expense of the core; moreover, "the best place to learn most jobs is on site." If vocational topics are good and engaging "stuff for learning," however, they can be used. Typing is an important skill which should be a school-wide requirement.

<u>Foreign language</u> study is usually defended to reduce isolationism and ethnocentrism, goals which can be well addressed in history; but a foreign language is a sensible elective for many students, except for one who is still struggling to learn his or her own language.

<u>Computer Literacy</u>: Like calculators and books, computers help students to learn; they are important as tools for learning, not in themselves.

● Skills are the heart of what should be taught: "reading, writing, speaking, listening, measuring, estimating, calculation, seeing—and the basic modes of imagining and of reasoning should...pervade all subjects...."

Sizer gives an example of the thought process involved in one skill:

> In seeing, or observing, "the trick is to decide what to record, which of the myriad data...is so important that its image should be retained...people who observe the same candle describe it differently....Each person's motives for looking will vary....A student needs to be aware of these inevitable discrepancies... and gain...self-consciousness in selecting.

He lists some of the other skills involved in the process of inquiry: knowing the difference between observation and inference; listening to someone talk and recasting in one's own words what was heard, including the speaker's visible signals; describing, which to be understandable must be precise and use a common terminology of words and symbols; complex thinking, which requires both remembering and juggling variables; analysis and resolution, which involves getting rid of unimportant variables, identifying and ordering the most important aspects of a problem, and identifying what is still unknown; application, using the idea, which involves making a decision that is often a leap of faith; learning to make an informed estimate, which helps in the decision and which is often discouraged by schools as guessing; and, finally, understanding, developing powers of discrimination, judging whether things are "good or bad"—all of which involve knowing the key questions to ask.

117

Everyone uses these processes intuitively but can learn to use them much more effectively. Schools can help by making the skills explicit; writing helps because it makes a record of the reasoning process for the student to review.

● Sizer also maintains that "any school of integrity... should try to help its students become decent people," decency being a combination of "fairness, generosity, and tolerance." Decency should be taught to students both directly and by example, by the way in which the school is run.

Methods

● For creating the setting for learning:

- Find the level at which a student is challenged yet can succeed. Make sure that every student is successful at something.

- Make it safe to make mistakes and help students use them for learning.

- Indicate by careful listening and summarizing that each student has important ideas to contribute.

● For helping students develop thinking skills:

- "Schools that always insist on the right answer, with no concern about how a student reaches it, smother the student's efforts to become an effective intuitive thinker"; instead, well-directed questions can redirect a student and promote more effective intuition.

- The only way to learn to think well is by practice, and a teacher assists by coaching--observing a student's work, pointing out strengths and failings, suggesting possible improvements, observing, and repeating the cycle.

- Questioning is needed to stimulate development of understanding and judgment--asking the key questions on both sides of an issue. Questioning requires a seminar format, a circle fewer than 20 people, give-and-take with the teacher being a participant as well as a leader. "Questioning is...far more difficult...for teachers than coaching and telling, because it is the least predictable"--a teacher cannot always control where it will go.

- Adjust work to each student's pace. "The personalization inherent in such adjusted pacing is also rewarding; it signals that the student is important as an individual."

Evaluation

● Students should be evaluated by final "exhibitions of mastery," which students can take when they are prepared to. "Effective exhibitions will be complicated to construct and time-consuming to administer. To be fair, they need to be flexible: not all students show themselves off well in the same way. They cannot, then, merely be standardized, machine-graded, paper-and-pencil tests."

School Organization

● A teacher should not be responsible for more than a total of 80 students. To achieve this student-teacher ratio, it may be worth breaking down disciplinary specializations. For example, it could be better if one teacher taught English and social studies to 60 students rather than just English to 120 different students.

● The current tracking system (honors, academic, general, technical, etc.) should be abolished, and students should develop at their own pace in each subject area. "It can be handled if the units (separate high schools, or "houses" within high schools) are kept small enough to allow a particular group of teachers to know particular students well and develop a track for each."

● "Personalization of learning and instruction requires a flexible school structure. A flexible structure implies a simple structure. A school day segmented into seven or eight time units, each with its own set of imperatives, is almost impossible to bend."

● Class sizes need to differ in terms of their purpose--larger for "telling," smaller for "coaching" and "questioning."

● Students who are consistently disruptive "should be expelled, with the same opportunities to return later as all dropouts have." Community colleges make return to schooling possible in many regions. Personalized alternative programs, however, may make dropout unnecessary.

● Decentralize school authority so that teachers and principals can adapt their schools to the needs, learning styles, and learning rates of their particular students.

● The public address system, office messengers, extracurricular and public relations exercises that interfere with teaching and learning should all be curtailed as they signal low priority for serious intellectual activity.

Teachers

● Training in teaching must be almost wholly school-based, with a good deal of coaching by experienced instructors.

● The best will have to be paid better; a more steeply scaled salary schedule is essential. There will have to be more variety within the teacher's career; traditional teaching must be mixed with periods of work as supervisor, counselor, developer of curriculum materials, and administrator.

Principals

● A principal should be the lead teacher; the business manager should be another executive. The principal must spend time with students and colleagues and make the decisions that affect the life of the school.

* * * * *

Sizer, Theodore R. Horace's Compromise: The Dilemma of the American High School. Boston: Houghton Mifflin, 1984. 241 pp. $16.95

Hampel, Robert C.; Cohen, David K.; and Farrar, Eleanor. Historical Essays on American High Schools Since 1940 (tentative title). Boston: Houghton Mifflin, forthcoming, Winter 1984.

Powell, Arthur G. The Shopping Mall High School. Boston: Houghton Mifflin, forthcoming, 1985.

A Study of High Schools, 18 Tremont Street, Boston, MA 02108

AN EDUCATION OF VALUE, initiated under the auspices of the National Academy of Education. The authors describe this book as "a thoughtful essay which attempts to engage the debate about the values and purposes of American education, and to consider the process by which these might be achieved." An Education of Value maintains that education in a democracy must aim for both excellence and equality: equality to give all citizens the skills necessary for thoughtful and active citizenship, and excellence ranging from the basic skills of literacy and problem solving, to creative and critical thinking, to the desire to further expand one's knowledge and skills.

The book is divided into three parts. Part I, "Recurring Priorities, Recurring Tensions," examines the expectations Americans have held for the school, how ambitious these expectations have been, and how they have changed over time. Part II, "The Purpose of Schooling," examines equality and excellence. It shows how the shift in education from a nineteenth-century concern with moral and political aims to a twentieth-century concern with economic roles "sharpened the conflict between equality and educational excellence at costs to both." It defines learning as involving intellect, emotions, intuition, and will, and challenges the view that the schools ought first to teach basic skills and only later more creative and sophisticated skills. Part III, "Learning and Teaching," examines teaching, the curriculum, the entrance of microcomputers as a case study in education, and the implications of these factors for the twin goals of excellence and equality. This section concludes with a reform agenda beginning with the proposition that reform

121

must start by empowering teachers, principals, and other educators to improve their own teaching and learning.

* * * * *

Lazerson, Marvin; McLaughlin, Judith Block; McPherson, Bruce; and Bailey, Stephen. <u>An Education of Value</u>. New York: Cambridge University Press, forthcoming, 1985.

POLICY OPTIONS FOR QUALITY EDUCATION, a report of the Task Force on Education Quality of the National Association of State Boards of Education (NASBE). The NASBE Task Force examined recommendations offered by recent reports on schooling and then offered its own policy recommendations, which are intended to emphasize those issues over which State Boards of Education have influence and which are most critical to achieving the goal of excellence in education. Although this report is directed to state boards, we include this summary to inform local planners of what states are being asked to do. Recommendations are offered in four areas:

Teacher Workforce Quality

"State boards should improve the quality of the teacher workforce by enacting policies to recruit and retain more effective teachers, improve the quality of teacher training, screen out and remove incompetent teachers, and reward teaching excellence.

"Recommendation 1. To increase the pool of highly qualified candidates entering the teaching profession, state boards should experiment with a host of financial incentives, including: an across-the-board increase in teacher compensation; mechanisms that reward teaching excellence; and a system of college scholarships, loans, and tuition reductions.

"Recommendation 2. To ensure that only qualified teachers are hired, prospective teachers should be given rigorous tests of competence in subject matter and pedagogical knowledge. In addition, they should be required to serve a period of internship. Once employed, teachers

122

should be periodically reevaluated. A Bachelor's degree and satisfactory performance on objective tests of competence should be preprequisites for employment; however, policies should be developed to qualify persons with relevant work experience of background, similar to current policies for teachers of vocational education.

"Recommendation 3. States should institute a systematic review of all teacher training programs and repeat the review in three- to five-year cycles. Review should focus on: (1) raising standards for admission to teacher-training programs; (b) placing greater emphasis on subject-matter competence; (c) providing opportunities for students and faculty to gain valuable hands-on experience by interacting closely with on-the-job teachers and administrators; (d) retraining displaced or surplus teachers to fill shortages in particular areas of the curriculum."

Academic Standards

"Academic standards must be raised at all grade levels for students of widely ranging abilities. Student performance that goes well beyond minimum standards must be encouraged through programs that respond to the diverse interests and abilities of the student population. In raising standards, state boards must review recently purchased textbooks, software, and other teaching materials to ensure that they reflect new, higher academic standards.

"Recommendation 1. In order to raise minimum achievement standards, two courses of action are recommended: adoption of a rigorous core curriculum, and implementation of student testing for diagnosis and remedial and other assistance.

"Recommendation 2. Schools cannot be satisfied with minimum competence. State boards should mandate kindergarten for all children, with special attention to students who are less likely to attain reading readiness in regular programs. State boards should support efforts to establish a variety of programs for special students, including the gifted and students with interests in science and the arts. Attention to the special educational needs of children who are disadvantaged, handicapped, or have limited proficiency in English must be continued to ensure equal opportunity for all.

"Implementation of a core curriculum requires that state board members identify subject-matter areas that all students are expected to complete, and specify a minimum number of instructional hours. State boards should also establish a system of assessing student outcomes based on the concepts of minimum competence and mastery learning. Any system of testing should be accompanied by a parallel effort to diagnose student deficiencies and provide appropriate remedial assistance. However, graduation from elementary education and from junior and senior high schools must rest on satisfactory completion of a core curriculum and demonstrated competence in its basic knowledge components.

"Higher academic standards must not be pursued at the expense of recent gains in educational equity and opportunity for all students. Officials must strive for a delicate balance between the common interests of our society and the diverse abilities of a heterogeneous student population. Non-college-bound students need appropriate vocational instruction, career counselling, and other preparation for success in the workplace."

School Organization

"State boards of education should challenge schools to create an environment for quality education by: (1) establishing programs to improve the leadership and management capabilities of the administrative force; and (2) providing guidance to districts in the adoption of policies and practices identified with educational excellence.

"Recommendation 1. State boards should define the knowledge and interpersonal skills that make for effective school principals and establish statewide principal certification requirements. Boards should help school districts design systems for periodically evaluating principals on the basis of competence, performance, schoolwide learner outcomes, and school-community relations.

"Recommendation 2. State boards should establish programs to improve the leadership and management capabilities of principals and other administrative personnel. Inservice education, summer institutes, and
periodic internships should be instituted to allow
exchange of information, including information on current
research, and to teach school leadership skills,
organizational dynamics, and personnel management
techniques.

"Recommendation 3. Administrative salaries do not
adequately recognize differences in performance. State
boards should encourage awards to administrators who
carry out major unit, school, or districtwide reforms.

"Recommendation 4. State boards should create statewide
programs to recognize effective schools. These programs
should adopt indicators of academic performance and
school environment, such as efficient and effective use
of instructional time and at-home learning; incentives
for appropriate classroom behavior; involvement of
teachers in school decisionmaking; broad and active
parent participation; active school-community
partnerships; and a broad range of activities on programs
that offer students many routes to achievement.

"Recommendation 5. State boards should continue or
expand efforts to encourage women and minorities to
compete for administrative positions."

Use of Time

"The Task Force places top priority on the effective use
of time already available in the school day and year.
Until existing resources are properly managed, proposals
to extend the school calendar are premature.

"Recommendation 1. State boards should set minimums for
the percentage of the school day during which students
must receive and teachers must provide instruction in
core subjects.

"Recommendation 2. State boards should establish
policies on student absenteeism that: (a) set minimum
attendance levels for promotion; and (b) require higher

levels of attendance for participation in extracurricular activities.

"Recommendation 3. State boards should ensure that state training and technical assistance activities provide guidance to school principals and other administrators on ways to increase effective use of instructional time."

* * * * *

Policy Options for Quality Education. Alexandria, Va.: National Association of State Boards of Education, 1984. 12 pp.

National Association of State Boards of Education, 701 North Fairfax Street, Suite 340, Alexandria, VA 22314

THE FAILURE OF OUR PUBLIC SCHOOLS: THE CAUSES AND A SOLUTION, issued in 1983 by the National Center for Policy Analysis (NCPA), a nonpartisan policy research institute based in Dallas. This report maintains that the basic problem with American public education lies in the fact that "since World War II, an increasing share of public school revenues has been awarded to school districts on the basis of student attendance" rather than academic achievement, thus encouraging school districts to engage in practices that will maximize their daily student attendance, a goal which often conflicts with learning goals. Furthermore, since the report maintains that there is no financial penalty attached to low academic achievement, school districts also have sacrificed learning goals to other, peripheral goals selected by principals, teachers, and students, for example, "developing a positive self-image." To rectify this situation, the NCPA proposes a new system for the financing of public schools that bases funding on academic achievement as well as on attendance.

* * * * *

The Failure of Our Public Schools: The Causes and a Solution. Dallas: National Center for Policy Analysis, 1983. 25 pp. $10.00

The National Center for Policy Analysis, 413 Carillon Plaza, 13601 Preston Road, Dallas, TX 75240

EDUCATION AND ECONOMIC PROGRESS: TOWARD A NATIONAL EDUCATION POLICY: THE FEDERAL ROLE, a statement that grew out of a meeting convened by the Carnegie Corporation in February 1983 to discuss the educational trends of an American economy dependent upon science and technology. The meeting involved 50 national leaders in government, business, labor, foundations, science, and education, and had two purposes: (1) to review the numerous current initiatives and reports on education, and (2) "to explore the desirability and feasibility of taking advantage of the current momentum to develop a coherent national policy linked to economic progress." Although this report is directed to the federal role, it is included here to inform local planners of what the federal government is being asked to do.

The conference "concluded that national leadership for a sustained period of time is essential to keep the nation's feet to the fire with respect to the need for educational improvement. Though the present emphasis should be upon mathematics, science, engineering, and foreign language skills, the conferees cited the need for qualitative improvement across the full spectrum of the humanities and social sciences as well."

A working group chaired by Governor James B. Hunt, Jr., of North Carolina, and Dr. David Hamburg, president of the Carnegie Corporation of New York, drafted Education and Economic Progress: Toward a National Education Policy: The Federal Role after analyzing current legislative proposals on educational reform. This working group came to the following conclusion:

> Better education for economic growth requires action at all levels of government--local, state, federal-- and in the private sector. The argument for federal action is that there is a pressing national need that the states and the private sector cannot meet alone. Moreover, with a mobile population and increasingly specialized economy the benefits of education accrue

127

to the nation as a whole and not to just any one state or locality. (p. 4)

The group recommended that federal legislation should:

● Serve two major purposes: improvement in mathematical and scientific literacy for the general population and development of high-level skills, including foreign language skills, among the most talented.

● Include three levels of education in a comprehensive approach: schools, colleges, and adult retraining.

● Build on state and local initiatives.

● Encourage partnerships among business/labor, education, and government.

● Support good programs already in operation as well as new programs aimed at reform.

● Emphasize talent development among minorities and women.

● Enlist the best scientific minds of the nation to work on school and college curriculum projects and teacher training.

● Recognize the dignity and worth of school and college teachers.

● Provide incentives to leverage and encourage state, local, and private investment in education.

● Build in a sustained federal role.

* * * * *

Education and Economic Progress: Toward a National Education Policy: The Federal Role. New York: Carnegie Corporation of New York, 1983. 15 pp.

Carnegie Corporation of New York, 437 Madison Avenue, New York, NY 10027

IMPROVING STUDENT PERFORMANCE IN CALIFORNIA: RECOMMENDA-
TIONS FOR THE CALIFORNIA ROUNDTABLE, a report of the
California Roundtable, an organization of senior execu-
tives of major California corporations "concerned that
the public schools might not be producing the educational
outcomes needed for a healthy society and economy." The
group commissioned Berman, Weiler Associates "to investigate the nature of the problem and what the California
business community could do to help." The recommendations in Improving Student Performance have been endorsed
nationally by the Business Roundtable in a "Paper on
Education," issued by its Employment Policy Task Force in
December 1983. The recommendations for business most
likely to interest local planners are that the business
community should:

● "Establish business expectations...business community
representatives should establish and disseminate to
schools and parents a description of the minimum skills
and competencies required for beginning employment."

● "Support the following government actions to raise
standards:
- Minimum graduation requirements
- Required local use of state curriculum guidelines
- Strengthened state testing of student performance
- Textbook upgrading
- Strengthened attendance and discipline laws
- Longer school day and year."

● "...help schools through the short-run math/science
emergency while more comprehensive state programs are
being developed. [Businesses could]:
- Release employees and encourage retiring employees to
teach math/science.
- Provide summer and part-time jobs for math/science
teachers.
- Make equipment and facilities available to schools."

● "Establish programs to help recruit and retain high
quality math/science teachers...:
- Provide scholarships and loans for prospective
math/science teachers.

129

- Establish dual career options for math/science teachers.
- Establish Teacher Fellowship programs for outstanding math/science teachers."

● "Increase community involvement:
-Conduct public information campaigns to increase parent/ community support for education.
-Provide releast time for parent-employees to do volunteer work in schools.
- Lend management experts to help improve schools' efficiency."

* * * * *

Improving Student Performance in California: Recommenda-tions for the California Roundtable. Berkeley: Berman, Weiler Associates, 1982. 83 pp. (An Executive Summary is also available.)

The California Roundtable, P.O. Box 7643, San Francisco, CA 94119-7643

"Paper on Education." 13 pp., Business Roundtable, 200 Park Avenue, New York, NY 10166

AGAINST MEDIOCRITY: THE HUMANITIES IN AMERICA'S HIGH SCHOOLS, edited by Chester E. Finn, Jr., Diane Ravitch, and Robert T. Fancher, a collection of essays that appraise the conditions of the humanities in the schools and propose approaches and curricula for high schools and for teacher education. This book arrived too late for us to review in depth and analyze with other studies, but we want to bring it to readers' attention because the essays bring a humanities perspective to a number of issues raised by the other studies and explore some new ones.

Examples of topics and issues—great and small—that may interest local education planners are:

● The role of the humanities in intellectual develop-ment.

- Some general approaches and activities for teaching about language and reasoning.
- A framework for an English curriculum that:
- Is organized around the crucial themes and questions of our culture.
- Educates the imagination.
- Teaches the skill of interpretation.

- The role of regional and ethnic dialects.

- The case for fluency in a foreign language.

- An approach to teaching history that:
- Establishes a sense of time and place.
- Examines the craft of historical research.
- Explores point of view.

- Textbooks versus original source materials.

- The intellectual lives of teachers.

* * * * *

Finn, Chester E., Jr.; Ravitch, Diane; and Fancher, Robert T., eds. Against Mediocrity: The Humanities in America's High Schools. New York: Holmes and Meier, 1984. 276 pp. $11.50

**Studies That Focus on Recommendations
for Improving the Education of College-Bound Students**

ON FURTHER EXAMINATION, the 1977 report of an advisory
panel set up by the College Board and chaired by Willard
Wirtz to investigate the then 14-year decline in Scholastic Aptitude Test scores. The panel reviewed the contemporary literature and commissioned studies on a wide
range of factors that had been proposed as possible influences in the decline.

The decline in Scholastic Aptitude Test scores is a major
piece of evidence that people cite in describing current
deficiencies in high school education. The College Board
panel's analysis of what the decline means and what factors may be responsible for it was discussed in chapter
two. Below are some of the panel's recommendations, ex-
cerpted from On Further Examination.

What Should Be Taught

"In our view, `returning to the basics' would be wrong
unless it included full reappraisal of what the right
basics are--taking account of children's different rates
and modes of learning and their different interests and
plans for the future. The need is not to revert to uniform drills and exercises commended only by a traditional
pedagogy, but to move ahead to a larger emphasis on the
fundamentals of learning....

"We would not recommend any single formulation of subject
matter or teaching method, for both traditional and innovative approaches to learning can produce good results--
or bad....

"We do not identify the score decline narrowly with reduced high school offerings of whatever used to be included in Advanced English courses. There is as much
opportunity and incentive for worthwhile reading and
writing in subject-matter areas of student interest.

"We attach central importance to restoring the traditions
of critical reading and careful writing....

132

"[See] to it that young people do more reading that
enhances vocabulary and enlarges knowledge and experience, and more writing that makes fledgling ideas test
and strengthen their wings....

"We can't prove that learning how to write is related to
a decline in scores on a test that required no writing.
Yet we suspect strongly that expressing something clearly
and correctly--especially in writing--is thinking's
sternest discipline."

The Impact of Television

"Particularly because of the impact of television...a
good deal more of most children's learning now develops
through viewing and listening than through traditional
modes. Little is known yet about the effects of this
change, including its relationship to performance levels
on standardized examinations.

"We surmise that the extensive time consumed by television detracts from homework, competes with schooling
more generally, and has contributed to the decline in SAT
score averages. Yet we are convinced that television and
related forms of communication give the future of
learning its largest promise. The most constructive
approach seems to us to depend less on limiting the uses
of these processes than it does on the willingness of the
community and the family to exercise the same responsibility for what is taught and learned this way as they
have exercised with respect to older forms of education."

* * * * *

On Further Examination: Report of the Advisory Panel on
the Scholastic Aptitude Test Score Decline. New York:
College Entrance Examination Board, 1977. 75 pp. $4.00

College Board Publications, Box 886, New York, NY 10101

THE ADVISORY COMMISSION ON ARTICULATION BETWEEN SECONDARY
EDUCATION AND THE OHIO COLLEGES, appointed in 1980 by the
Ohio Board of Regents and the Ohio Board of Education.

Its purpose was to develop "a college preparatory curriculum that will clearly reflect collegiate expectations for entering students, and, when followed, would reduce the need for remedial coursework at the collegiate level." This study was among the first of the current state efforts to design high school preparation to match college needs, a task relevant for all states. The recommendations that follow are adapted from more detailed ones to which teachers and curriculum supervisors may wish to refer.

What Should Be Taught

● <u>English</u>: Four years, with particular emphasis on writing skills, plus reading, listening, speaking, and research skills and the study of literature.

● <u>Mathematics</u>: Three years, including two years of algebra and geometry, one of which should be taken in the senior year.
- Courses should emphasize problem solving and grade on the display of problem-solving processes in clear stepwise fashion.
- Understanding of the versatility and limitations of the computer through firsthand experience with application to a variety of subjects, though not essential, is recommended.
- Students intending to enter fields requiring college calculus should take four years of high school math.

● <u>Science</u>: Three years, including at least two from among laboratory courses in earth science, biology, chemistry.
- "Science courses should serve as vehicles for the use and development of communication (i.e., reading, writing, and vocabulary development) and mathematical skills, while emphasizing observation, data collection and analysis, reasoning and critical thinking. As part of this effort, students should learn such skills as sequencing, making comparisons, and differentiating between facts and opinions."

● "Students who intend to pursue a baccalaureate degree in scientific fields should take four years of science to include biology, chemistry, and physics plus an advanced course, seminar, or research topic using an analytical approach in one science area."

● Social Studies: Three years, including one year of American history, one year of world history, and one year of American government combined with a choice among comparative government, problems of democracy, or specific social sciences such as economics, anthropology, geography, psychology, or sociology. World history should be taken in the senior year.

● Foreign Languages: Two years of a foreign language; three years of a foreign language for students whose college major requires language facility.

● Writing in General: "Teachers and administrators should develop curricula plans to encourage student writing on a daily basis....The evaluation of writing needs to be individualized."

Evaluation and Guidance

● College placement tests in math and English should be given to students in their junior year so that the results can be used to counsel them about senior year choices in math and English.

Teacher Education

● "Teacher certification requirements should reflect a greater emphasis on major subject matter content areas. This emphasis on content areas should also be carried over to inservice education as well as recertification requirements."

● "Teacher education activities and communications should emphasize the need for high school students to write more in all subjects and especially in English classes. In addition, teachers should enforce more rigorous work requirements in order to reduce grade inflation."

* * * * *

Report: Advisory Commission on Articulation Between Secondary Education and Ohio Colleges. Columbus, Ohio: Ohio State Board of Regents/State Board of Education, 1981. 20 pp.
Reports of the Task Forces on Science, Social Studies, and Foreign Languages. Columbus, Ohio: Ohio Board of Regents/State Board of Education, 1982. 11 pp.

State Board of Education, 808 Ohio Departments Building, 65 South Front Street, Columbus, OH 43215

Ohio Board of Regents, 3600 State Office Tower, 30 East Broad Street, Columbus, OH 43215

EDUCATIONAL EQUALITY PROJECT, a ten-year effort of the College Board to strengthen the quality of secondary education and to ensure equality of opportunity for post-secondary education. Begun in 1980, the project is under the direction of the Board's Office of Academic Affairs.

In 1983 the project issued Academic Preparation for College: What Students Need to Know and Be Able to Do, which is the result of meetings and dialogues involving more than 1,400 educators working to define the knowledge and skills that should be acquired in high school to meet the academic demands of college. The book provides an educational agenda for college-bound students.

Academic Preparation for College presents a comprehensive description of the knowledge and skills needed by all college entrants. It maintains that students should achieve Six Basic Competencies which "are the broad intellectual skills essential ·to effective work in all fields of college study." The Six Basic Academic Competencies are reading, writing, speaking and listening, mathematics, reasoning, and studying.

The study also recognizes that since computers are taking on greater importance, another needed competency is basic familiarity with how computers work, what they can be used for, and the social, economic, and ethical issues of their use.

136

Academic Preparation for College also describes what they need to learn in Six Basic Academic Subjects that provide the specific knowledge and skills on which college-level study is based.

● English, including reading and literature, speaking and listening, writing, and language.

● Arts, consisting of a general education in the arts and more intensive education in at least one of: the visual arts, theater, music, dance.

● Mathematics, including computers, statistics, algebra, geometry, functions; prospective science or engineering majors should have more extensive preparation in mathematics.

● Science, including laboratory and field work, mathematical skill, fundamental concepts, detailed knowledge in at least one scientific field: either physics, biology, chemistry, one of the earth sciences, one of the new interdisciplinary fields.

● Social studies, including a knowledge of history, geography, and cultures, and of social science methodology.

● Foreign languages, enough for proficiency in another language and culture.

Space limitations prevent us from examining either the Basic Academic Subjects or Competencies in detail. Those interested in their specific content should refer to chapters two, three, and four of Academic Preparation for College.

Although the major emphasis of this College Board project is on the importance of the Basic Academic Competencies and Subjects, it also voices other concerns relating to a quality college-preparatory high school program.

The commitment, sustained effort, and creativity of local schools will be crucial to improving the prep-aration of college-bound students. Teachers and administrators will have to consider carefully and

137

work out curriculum and instructional approaches to achieving these learning outcomes.

[High school counselors] will have an important role to play in achieving these outcomes. They can explain the connection of these outcomes—and the effort needed to achieve them—to success in college study. Counselors can help build a climate of encouragement and expectation that will motivate students to persist in a strong program of academic preparation for college.

The overall environment created in the schools is an important part of achieving these outcomes. Students learn best when excellence is expected of them and when they are encouraged to achieve it. They need incentives and stimulation to learning. Students will achieve these learning outcomes most readily when instruction is keyed to the stages of their intellectual development.

Students will need to bear in mind the effect of their own attitude on the learning process and on their schools. They will need a sense of personal responsibility for their own progress and a desire to make full use of their teachers as resources. They must be ready to conduct themselves in ways that make learning possible for their classmates as well as for themselves. (pp. 31-33)

* * * * *

Academic Preparation for College: What Students Need to Know and Be Able to Do. New York: The College Board, 1983. 46 pp.

Multiple copies are available in packages of 20 for $20. Orders of 5 or more packages receive a 20% discount. Payment or a purchase order should be addressed to College Board Publications, Department A35, Box 886, New York, NY 10101.

The College Board, Office of Academic Affairs, 888 Seventh Avenue, New York, NY 10106 (212-582-6210)

**Studies That Focus on What Does and Does Not Work
in Existing Programs to Provide Educational Excellence**

MEETING THE DEVELOPMENTAL NEEDS OF THE EARLY COLLEGE STUDENT, a report on the approach of Simon's Rock of Bard College by Nancy Goldberger. Simon's Rock "accepts capable 10th and 11th grade students into a college liberal arts program characterized by small classes, extensive contact with faculty, and opportunities for independent work on and off campus."

Simon's Rock and other "early college" programs are part of a movement that advocates restructuring American education in the following directions:

● Elimination of the traditional structure that pre-scribes four years of secondary school previous to admission to college, a system that violates the tenet that people learn at different rates and have different aptitudes.

● The development of a national policy that would let students enter college because of their readiness rather than their chronological age.

Building on developmental theories that view adolescent development on dimensions such as absolutism to rela-tivism and conformity to post-conformity, Goldberger recommends the following for colleges for younger students. They may be relevant for high schools as well:

● The most valuable learning takes place when the student is able to take an active part in the classroom process, challenging and being challenged by others, participating in group problem-solving, dreaming up and testing hypotheses. The large lecture class, with little opportunity for questions, let alone discussion, is developmentally disastrous for some students.

● The most productive learning takes place in situations characterized by dynamic interaction between teacher and student and by practical experience with the subject matter. When students can meet faculty informally out-side of class (for discussion or recreation), "the knowl-edge and teaching/learning style that the teacher represents in the student's eyes will come to seem less abstract."

● "The common goal is to help students move away from simplistic, absolutist thinking, and away from the `multiplistic dilemma' of believing that all opinions are equally valid, a position leading to irresponsibly subjective choices: `What feels right to me.' Stated positively, the educational goal is...`contextual relativism,' a recognition that difficult questions have multiple answers but that within such relativism one can nonetheless make reasonable choices and formulate enduring commitments."

● Important "from a faculty point of view...are the special weekly meetings of teachers from the arts, humanities, social and natural sciences....conversation moves from critiques of specific assignments (to assess their likelihood of encouraging student development) to discussion of student writing problems that may be developmentally based to more abstract speculation about teaching strategies and styles...."

* * * * *

Goldberger, Nancy. <u>Meeting the Developmental Needs of the Early College Student: The Simon's Rock Experiment.</u> May 1980.

Nancy Goldberger, Austen Riggs Center, Inc., Stockbridge, MA 01262.

<u>A Case for Educational Restructuring.</u> Great Barrington, Mass.: Simon's Rock of Bard College, 1981. 94 pp.
Available from Susan Van Kleeck, Simon's Rock of Bard College, Great Barrington, MA 01230

THE WALLS WITHIN: WORK, EXPERIENCE, AND SCHOOL REFORM, a study conducted for the Huron Institute by Eleanor Farrar, John E. DeSanctis, and Peter Cowden of the implementation of Experience-Based Career Education (EBCE), September 1980. EBCE is a high school school-and-work program developed by four regional educational laborato-

140

ries under the auspices of the National Institute of Education. The Walls Within, a three-year study of the implementation of this program, examined 45 programs using field-based interviews and observations.

The Walls Within is included here because it addresses two approaches recommended by many of the current studies: bringing business and the community into education roles, and individualizing instruction. Following are excerpts from the report:

"Experience-Based Career Education attempted to put into practice some theories about school, the community, and the best preparation for life. It was developed in response to U.S. Education Commissioner Sidney Marland's career education initiative. It not only aspired to break down the barriers between school and life by putting youth out in the community, but it also proposed to intervene in traditional school practices so that employers and community organizations could participate in the academic as well as the work-related education of teenagers.

"EBCE, like earlier reform programs, has produced little substantial change in high schools, their pedagogy and curriculum, or student behavior. Yet the program has been widely adopted and immensely popular. It enabled many community, staff, and student participants to satisfy a wide range of personal and professional needs, but it also provided some evidence on the barriers to providing students with instructive and meaningful experiences through their exposure to work and community."

Integrating Academics and Experience: One major goal, blending experiential learning with academic, proved hard to realize. Since this is not a goal emphasized by current studies, we will not go into detail here.

The Work Experience in the Community: "Experience-Based Career Education called for a new kind of relationship between school and community--a balanced partnership not previously tried in American education.

"...While employers were willing to participate in such a program, it was not to the extent hoped for....It had

141

been intended that, in addition to teaching students about work through experience, employers would assume responsibility for providing academic instruction; and this they were not willing to do. Another problem concerned the wish to place students at the work site for the entire school day. This was opposed by employers for fear that regular employees might view the student as a threat, especially in jobs for which they might have the requisite skills, such as clerical and trade occupations. Finally, EBCE would have to compete with the wide range of existing vocational programs that already demanded employer cooperation and commitment.

"The limited success of the partnership suggests that there may be a fallacy in the underlying assumptions of the reform. Early EBCE advocates seemed to believe not only that it was a natural--if neglected--function of the community to help schools prepare youth for life, but also that the community would be eager to `reclaim its crucial role in preparing young people to live and work' in today's world. Yet the EBCE experience suggests that on the contrary, most Americans still expect schools to do that job."

<u>Individualizing Instruction</u>: "In seeking to reform the pedagogic process, the unit of change for EBCE was the individual student. Different students would have different out-of-school experiences, and so the experiential component of the curriculum would vary from student to student. And since each student's academic needs would also be unique, different academic components would result. Individual projects were therefore needed to accomodate a wide range of site experiences, personal interests, basic skills, and credit requirements....

"Rather than large-group, textbook-oriented classrooms, EBCE was to use a more flexible pedagogy of one-on-one teacher-student interactions and small group sessions, self-paced individual basic skills programs for academic weaknesses, and the availability of academic, career, and personal counseling.

"A typical EBCE teacher...met with each student at least one weekly, and...individual and small-group settings... were the rule in EBCE....

142

"...Students and teachers described one of the program's strongest attractions...[as] `the opportunity to work one-on-one with students on a range of subjects.' Many cited a long-standing belief that high school education should be more personal.... A learning coordinator...saw individual attention as the real strength of the program because it `gave the students a chance to realize that they were somebody and that they had assets and abilities which they could do something with.'"

"[Students] all seemed to `like the individual attention' best, in contrast to regular school, where, a student claimed, `the teachers never used to even know my name—but here they all know it and they like to try and make an appointment with you.' A student who had a history of problems with authority explained that the program was different in that the learning coordinators were `easier to talk to, there is more one-to-one attention, they're a lot cooler, and they expect things.' Generally, students seemed very conscious of the difference between EBCE and regular school...":

> It's different because we're not required to do stuff on schedule; also in the classes we have a lot more time to discuss. When there are big classes nobody can say more than one or two things, and usually people don't say anything and a couple of people dominate the conversation. Or maybe there really isn't any discussion at all. Also, you don't have to leave class when the bell rings, so that if you've got a really good discussion going you can just keep on going.

"Some students reported that their grades had improved and attributed the change to the increased attention from teachers. A young woman, asked why she was doing so much better in school, responded, `I understand my work better, because [the EBCE teacher] explains it to me. In regular school, if you don't get it, you just have to bear it.'

"Another explanation for improved grades was offered by a math teacher."

> There's a special chemistry that begins to operate in these teaching situations. Students don't have to do their work in classroom situations, where they can easily sit at the back of the class and fall rapidly

143

behind. But when teachers and students are working in a one-to-one situation...students feel more obligated to get their work done so that the lessons can proceed.

Managing Students: "In many districts, EBCE enabled schools to deal with disruptive students and those with chronic learning problems. It got students out of regular classes where they made trouble and into self-contained groups isolated from the rest of the school; it provided individual attention and counseling in personal matters, defusing much disruptive behavior or preventing it from getting out of hand; it offered individual instruction and tutoring to guide and monitor student progress toward academic credits and diplomas; and it placed students in the community, away from the familiar constraints of the school.

"These solutions would not have been possible within the context of the traditional school. By drawing from classes and into the program, schools could circumvent many of the rules and practices meant to apply uniformly to all students. Thus, for example, schools could provide tailor-made academic help or adjust the content of required courses to help some students graduate, which they could not have done for those same students in regular classes. Or they could sharply reduce the required hours of attendance at the school for EBCE students--to as little as two or three hours per week for limited times in some programs--without jeopardizing their official student status of diplomas. The regulations and rules once devised to protect student youth from society --compulsory attendance, required courses and credits-- had limited administrators' freedom of action in solving school and district problems. EBCE allowed them to bypass these constraints in a manner both public and legitimate."

Relations Between School and Community: "Another source of EBCE's appeal to districts was its expressive value. Because EBCE was advertised as a solution to academic problems as well as an introduction to work and careers, its adoption demonstrated to the community that the district was committed to dealing seriously with these matters. EBCE appeared to respond to both the uproar about

144

basic skills and the crisis of youth unemployment, and so met districts' ever-present concern about their image in the community. The schools' initiative to involve local businesses and employers with education also enhanced community relations. Employers were left with the impression that the schools were more accessible and, more important, that they depended upon the community to improve the quality of education. In at least the symbolic sense, this shifted some of the responsibility for education from the schools to the community. According to district staff, employers, and parents, many of those who had been hostile or indifferent to the schools developed a more favorable attitude, largely owing to their contact with the schools through the program."

* * * * *

For information about publications on this project, contact the Huron Institute, 123 Mount Auburn Street, Cambridge, MA 02138.

THE EFFECTIVE SCHOOLS MOVEMENT, an outgrowth of work led largely by the late Ronald Edmonds. He, and others engaged in this work, have maintained, contrary to the popularly held belief that family background and home environment are principal factors in pupil performance, that the character and effectiveness of the school can determine how much a student learns, especially in the area of basic academic skills.

The Effective Schools Movement has had three major phases. The first phase (1973-81) encompassed a project directed by Edmonds called Search for Effective Schools: The Identification and Analysis of City Schools That Are Instructionally Effective for Poor Children. This project attempted to answer the question, "Are there any schools in which acquisition of basic school skills is relatively independent of pupil membership in a social class subset?" The emphasis on low-income children was a result of Edmonds's concern with educational equity and desire to disprove theories that put the responsibility for ineffective education primarily on low-income parents.

145

Professor Edmonds concluded that there were schools that do an effective job of educating students regardless of family background, and that five characteristics are generally associated with such schools:

● Strong administrative leadership: a principal who is a strong instructional leader.

● School climate conducive to learning: an atmosphere that is orderly without being rigid or oppressive.

● High expectations that children can learn: expectations on the part of all school staff that do not permit a child to fall below minimal levels of mastery.

● A strong basic skills program: emphasis on the teaching of basic skills by a well-prepared teacher in teacher-directed classrooms where students spend most of their time on tasks.

● Ongoing assessment program: a procedure for frequent monitoring of all pupil programs.

A second phase in the Effective Schools Movement was the School Improvement Project, sponsored by the New York City Board of Education and directed by Edmonds, who was then the Senior Assistant to the Chancellor for Instruction. It aimed to clarify the factors that contribute to academic performance, to develop instruments to measure these factors in schools, and to develop school-improvement strategies based on the five characteristics.

At the same time, several other school systems were experimenting with improvement projects based on materials developed by the Searching for Effective Schools project. These included Project RISE in Milwaukee, Project SHAL in St. Louis, and the New Jersey Education Association School Effectiveness Training Project.

Since the death of Professor Edmonds, the Effective Schools Movement has continued as a series of reform programs. They include the Glendale (Arizona) Effective Schools project and the Illinois School Improvement Consortium. Professor Edmonds's colleagues have written a guide to the principles of the Effective Schools Movement, <u>Creating Effective Schools</u>. The movement's efforts are coordinated through a journal, <u>The Effective School Report</u>, which reports on implementation and research, and also through the Council for Effective Schools.

* * * * *

Brookover, Wilber B. et al. <u>Creating Effective Schools: An Inservice Program for Enhancing School Learning Climate and Achievement</u>. Holmes, Fla.: Learning Publications, 1982. 290 pp. $17.95

<u>The Effective School Report</u>. New York: Kelwynn, Inc., Monthly. $24/year. Available from: The Effective School Report, Kelwynn, Inc., Grand Central Station, P.O. Box 2058, New York, NY 10163

THE UNIVERSITY/URBAN SCHOOLS NATIONAL TASK FORCE, chaired by Richard M. Bossone, university dean for instructional research at the Graduate School of the City University of New York. This group organized a series of five conferences to share information about problems and solutions in urban education. Each conference has resulted in a volume on the proceedings.

Volume I contains papers on "Achievement Goals Program for Reading and Mathematics: Grades 1-6," "School Improvement Programs in New York City," and "Mission Excellence: A Diagnostic/Prescriptive Approach to an Individualized Instructional Program." Volume II includes papers on "The Reform of an Urban School System: The San Francisco Redesign Program," "Historical Perspective on Educational Technology," "Improving Basic Skills: Factors to Consider," and "Techniques to Raise Urban Students' Standings on Standardized Tests." Volume III describes specific school improvement experiences in the Minneapolis, Detroit, and St. Louis school systems. Volume IV contains papers on four programs designed to improve both learning abilities needed for academic work and reasoning skills. Volume V focuses on such school reform issues as education and politics, schools and universities, and instruction and learning.

Several of the papers are of particular interest because they offer examples of successful approaches in areas designated by other studies as needing help, such as:

- Methods for teaching thinking and reasoning skills.

- Methods for teaching basic skills that respond to individual learning problems and styles.

- Methods that work for improving large urban schools.

* * * * *

For information on this program, contact Dean Richard M. Bossone, Graduate School of the City of New York, 33 West 42nd Street, New York, NY 10036

HIGH SCHOOL AND BEYOND, a longitudinal survey of American high school sophomores and seniors conducted for the National Center for Educational Statistics by the National Opinion Research Center of the University of Chicago. Its primary purpose is the observation of "the educational and occupational plans and activities of young people as they pass through the American educational system and take on their adult roles." The base-year survey (Spring 1980) included over 30,000 sophomores and 28,000 seniors enrolled in 1,015 public and private high schools. In addition to questionnaires and cognitive tests for students, surveys were conducted among administrators, teachers, twins of students in the sample, and a sample of parents of student subjects. Survey results, as well as technical reports on specific topics such as youth employment, discipline, and Hispanic students, are available. Two notable book-length studies use the survey data:

High School Achievement: Public, Catholic, and Private Schools Compared, by James S. Coleman, Thomas Hoffer, and Sally Kilgore, concludes that private schools produce better cognitive outcomes than public schools (and that there may be unmeasured factors in the self-selection into the private sector that account for this); that private schools provide a safer, more disciplined envi-

148

ronment than public schools; and that private schools are primarily academic and lack the vocational and technical programs that public high schools often provide. The study maintains that academic demands and school discipline are closely related and that higher standards in these areas tend to be reflected in academic achievement. Authority (and thus discipline) in the public schools has been decreasing at least partially as a consequence of the weakening of other forms of authority (such as parental and religious authority). Private schools have more leeway than public schools in imposing both discipline and academic standards, and legal requirements do not constrain the private school to retain any particular student.

> ...private high schools tend to differ from schools in the public sector in a number of ways. They operate in a different relation to parents, who have spent money to enroll their child in the school and thus can be expected to be more involved with the schools and to reinforce the school's demands. They operate in a different relation to their students, who know the school is not required to keep them. They generally impose greater academic demands and maintain stronger standards of discipline. They are usually smaller, and most of them operate on less money per pupil than does the average public school....

> ...Comparing the outcomes...will suggest differences to look for among schools, whether in the public sector or the private sector, in the search for factors affecting achievement. (pp. xxvii-xxviii)

Catholic High Schools and Minority Students, by Andrew M. Greeley, uses the base-year data to explore one problem: "Why black and Hispanic students who attend Roman Catholic schools display much higher levels of academic effort and achievement than black and Hispanic young people attending public schools." The study concludes that although part of the explanation lies in the fact that minority students who attend Catholic schools have very different family backgrounds and personal characteristics from those who do not, much of the achievement of the students is due to "the superior quality of Catholic schools," especially "the superior quality of academic instruction."

* * * * *

Coleman, James S.; Hoffer, Thomas; and Kilgore, Sally. High School Achievement: Public, Catholic, and Private Schools Compared. New York: Basic Books, 1982. 289 pp. $20.75

Greeley, Andrew M. Catholic High Schools and Minority Students. New Brunswick, N.J.: Transaction Books, 1982. 117 pp. $14.95

High School and Beyond: Information for Users, Base Year (1980) Data. Washington, D.C.: National Center for Educational Statistics, U.S. Department of Education. Room 600, Brown Building, 400 Maryland Avenue, SW, Washington, DC 20208

THE PROJECT ON ALTERNATIVES IN EDUCATION, directed by Mary Anne Raywid, founded in 1976 to encourage high school reform through research into alternative forms of secondary education. The project located and published a listing of over 2500 alternative secondary schools. It also conducted a survey of 1200 of these schools and published the results in 1982 as The Current Status of Schools of Choice in Public Secondary Education. This survey found that alternative schools were a thriving phenomenon that produced high staff morale, better student-teacher relations, and a higher attendance rate than mainstream high schools, at no additional cost.

"Advice Sheets" developed by the project give more detailed findings and recommendations, from which the following highlights have been adapted:

● Schools of choice provide diversity in public education; they exist in varying types as a well-established component of school districts.

● For all types of students, marginal to outstanding, alternative schools seem to produce significant

150

cognitive, social, and affective growth and achievement. Attendance and behavior of students also improve.

● Schools of choice are an effective response to student apathy, underachievement, truancy, and behavior problems; to staff burnout; to difficulties brought about by desegregation; and to the challenge of improving school quality.

● By comparison with other classes, alternative school classrooms are well ordered and reflect high degrees of task orientation and student involvement. This is accomplished with a minimum of teacher control. Alternative schools manage to personalize the school environment, rendering the school a genuine community.

The following components are important to successful programs for high-risk students:

What Should Be Taught

● A core curriculum of integrated studies jointly designed by the school staff. The integrating principle can be issues, themes, or problems, but it should organize otherwise separate and unconnected disciplines. This kind of organization helps students apply what they learn in one discipline to material in another, and to see the connections between the personal and the world that is public and shared.

● A developmental program designed to cultivate abstract thinking ability (to foster intellectual growth) along with personal and social maturation.

● A self-knowledge dimension to help students understand their own beliefs and potential, and, simultaneously, help them shift from a self-centered perspective and experience themselves as responsible members of a group.

Methods

● Independent study and experiential learning with detailed arrangements for internships or observations and classroom follow-through adding a reflective component.

• An academic program planned to permit early and frequent success.

• An academic agenda that is developmental as well as substantive. Staff should be willing to undertake remedial work but not make it a permanent compromise. These efforts are essential to avoid tracking, to maintain the self-esteem of students, and to avoid stigma outside the program.

• Adaptation of material to individual needs, along with group work and cooperative learning strategies such as team learning and peer tutoring.

• Explicit, achievable academic goals with short-term rewards. Broad, long-term goals must be broken down into specific, short-range, feasible subgoals in the form of individual competencies to be mastered, "contracts" to be fulfilled, or unit obligations to be met.

School Organization

• Concerted, continuing effort to generate a strong sense of affiliation on the part of the students. Schools for marginal students must be "membership schools" which youngsters feel they have joined. "Community-building" activities involving everyone should be scheduled regularly.

* * * * *

Raywid, Mary Anne. The Current Status of Schools of Choice in Public Secondary Education. Hempstead, N.Y.: Project on Alternatives in Education, Hofstra University, 1982. 36 pp.

Project on Alternatives in Education, c/o Mary Anne Raywid, Hofstra University, Hempstead, NY 11550

WHAT MAKES A GOOD SCHOOL? by Gerald Grant, Syracuse University, 1981. This study explores why schools differ in climate or ethos and how a climate or ethos conducive to education can be created. Grant uses the terms "climate" and "ethos" to denote both "the conditions under which learning takes place and...the way in which we establish these conditions." During the 1979-80 school year this project observed five schools that "exhibited a strong ethos or...where the adult leadership was consciously trying to effect a change in the climate." Findings on these schools were published as What Makes a Good School? Five Case Studies, an appendix to the project's major report, Education, Character, and American Schools: Are Effective Schools Good Enough?

Grant criticizes "effective schools research" for defining "effectiveness" by students' performance on standardized tests and ignoring issues of "social character." For Grant, the ethos or climate of a school is the most important determinant of the educational outcomes to be achieved. His conceptual framework is based on conclusions reached by Michael Rutter in his landmark study of several London schools, Fifteen Thousand Hours. Grant cites the characteristics that Rutter's study found to be true of the ethos of schools in which there was better conduct, lower delinquency, and higher achievement:

Teachers

● Teachers expected students to do well on exams.

● They regularly assigned and marked homework (which turned out to be much more important than the amount of time pupils spent on homework).

● They expected pupils to act responsibly and gave an opportunity to do so through...quasi-supervisory positions.

● They conveyed their expectations in the way they themselves behaved...(they were) punctual, started lessons on time, taught a full period.

● They frequently praised pupils' work.

● They took pupils on outings.

• Along with other staff, they were willing to see pupils at any time about a problem, not just during stated hours.

Schools

• The school had consistency and shared norms, although they differed from one another on their goals (which ranged from helping students develop their personalities to preparing them for a job).

• They were generally fair and consistent about standards and penalties for transgressing them (which matters more than specific forms of punishment).

• They provided joint planning opportunities for teachers.

Grant suggests three levels at which ethos can be altered to improve not only the social character of a school but educational outcomes as well:

Leadership: Principals and teachers must see the school as a moral and intellectual community; they must understand the nature of their authority, expect conflict, and seek to resolve it by showing their mutual interests and shared values. They must have the autonomy to make needed changes. Teachers should be sought by offering new incentives, including higher salary, liberal sabbatical policy, more collegial and learning opportunities, and a voice in teacher hiring.

Students: A "core of able students" is essential to the formation of a positive ethos.

Structure: Authority must be reestablished without losing recent gains in equity and without resorting to "a legalistic ethos" or "bureaucratic regulation." Toward this end, Grant suggests that school organization tend toward "the formulation of smaller and more humane schools." He also proposes radically reducing layers of bureaucracy, deflating incentives for bureaucratic careers, and giving more incentives for volunteerism and diversity through voucher plans for funding.

154

All improvements require a shared "provisional morality" which includes "the minimal order required for dialogue, the willingness to listen to others, respect for truth, the rejection of racism (or openness to participation in the dialogue), as well as those transcendent values which shore up the whole society: a sense of altruism and service to others, and respect for personal effort and hard work."

* * * * *

Grant, Gerald. Education, Character, and American Schools: Are Effective Schools Good Enough?   Syracuse, N.Y.: Syracuse University, 1981. 155 pp.

_____. What Makes a Good School? Five Case Studies. Syracuse, N.Y.: Syracuse University, 1981. 245 pp.

_____. "The Character of Education and the Education of Character," Daedalus, Summer 1981, pp. 135-50.

_____. "The Elements of a Strong Positive Ethos," National Association of Secondary School Principals Bulletin, March 1982, pp. 84-90.

_____. "The Teacher's Predicament," Teachers College Record, Spring 1983, pp. 593-609.

Rutter, Michael et al. Fifteen Thousand Hours: Secondary Schools and Their Effects on Children. Cambridge Mass.: Harvard University Press, 1979. 285 pp. $5.95

Dr. Gerald Grant, Cultural Foundations and Curriculum School of Education, Syracuse University, 259 Huntington Hall, Syracuse, NY 13210

THE GOOD HIGH SCHOOL: PORTRAITS OF CHARACTER AND CULTURE, by Sara Lawrence Lightfoot, Professor at Harvard Graduate School of Education, a series of in-depth "portraits" of six high schools (urban, suburban, and private preparatory schools) chosen because of their "goodness": "Exemplary schools that might tell us something about the myriad definitions of educational success and how it is achieved." The data for these portraits was gathered by intensive observation at each school, interviews with students, administrators, and teachers, and through reviews of school newspapers, student literary journals, school catalogs, and faculty and administrative documents.

Lightfoot found that there are a number of factors that contribute to "goodness" in high schools:

● "...good high schools reveal a sustained and visible ideological stance that guards them against powerful and shifting societal intrusions."

● Leadership, while often being perceived as solitary and masculine, "is fueled by partnerships and alliances with intimate, trusted associates" and exhibits "qualities traditionally identified as female—nurturance, receptivity, [and] responsiveness to relationships and context."

● Teachers are offered "the opportunity for autonomous expression, a wide angle on organizational participation and responsibility, and a degree of protection against the distorted social stereotypes that plague their profession."

● Teachers "know individual students well and are knowledgeable about adolescence as a developmental period," a knowledge that is expressed in their comfortable interactions with their students and their interpretation of, and response to, deviant acts.

● The institutional authority structures are coherent and sturdy, giving support and legitimacy to the disciplinary gestures of teachers.

● Attention is paid to "the rationale, coherence, and integrity of their academic curriculum" as well as to resolving "the perceived tensions between equity among student groups and the quality of academic pursuits."

● Students feel "visible and accountable."

* * * * *

156

Lightfoot, Sara Lawrence. The Good High School:
Portraits of Character and Culture. New York: Basic
Books, 1983. 399 pp. $19.95

SUCCESSFUL SCHOOLS FOR YOUNG ADOLESCENTS, by Joan
Lipsitz, Center for Early Adolescence at the University
of North Carolina. Dr. Lipsitz spent months observing
the characteristics of successful schools for 10- to 14-
year-olds. She views the needs posed by "the massive
individual differences in development" of this age group
as a major challenge. The report describes how four
successful schools meet these needs and gives these
common characteristics.

What Should Be Taught, and Method

Lipsitz does not emphasize curricular content, claiming,
in fact, that "it is not curriculum that raises these
schools from the mundane."

> Translating philosophy into curriculum is the most
> difficult feat for schools....translation to climate
> and organizational structure appears to be much
> easier....

> The strongest area of responsiveness is...[that these
> schools] meet the developmental diversity of the age
> group with comparable diversity in program....[They]
> have learned the importance of flamboyance in school-
> ing for young adolescents....What at first looks like
> spectacle is also solid curriculum and pedagogy that
> derives from a confident, often intuitive understand-
> ing of what playful, group-oriented, curious young
> adolescents need. (pp. 188-89)

School Organization

● The schools are responsive—they show a "willingness
and ability to adapt all school practices to the individual differences in intellectual, biological, and social
maturation...." Examples of adapting are: in one school
Friday is kept for mini-courses so that students can pursue personal interests; in another the school day is con-

157

structed around an advisory structure that allows every student "daily contact with an adult who has time to listen, explain, comfort, and prod."

● The approach to order and discipline is preventive and consists of practices (described below) that personalize the environment, foster continuity in relationships, and bind students to the school culture.

● Students have many routes for rewards. In addition to the usual academics and interscholastic teams, in which only a small percentage excell, there are arts, crafts, community service, camping trips, simulations, and intramural sports involving hundreds of students.

● The schools are organized into a "house" and "team" structure with no more than 150 students to a house. Every student is known by a team of teachers, and a common planning period allows teachers to consult with each other about individual students. The way each of the four schools achieved this type of organization is different.

Teachers

● Flexibility of school organization allows teachers to "vary the tone and pace of the day as needed."

● "The common planning period also promotes collegiality and professionalism in curriculum development and review."

Principals

● Principals should have a "driving vision" of school for this age group; derive their authority from acknowledged competence; see their major function as instructional leadership; secure the autonomy of their school and take an independent, aggressive approach to hiring and firing; and educate the community about schooling for this age group.

Evaluation

● "Standardized achievement tests appear to be playing a positive role" as they have documented "the need to commit time and staff to continued reading and math instruction."

School and Community

● Neighborhood or rational feeder patterns help because the school can belong to a self-identified community. Because schools are responsible to their communities, excellence leads to heterogeneity in schooling.

* * * * *

Lipsitz, Joan. Successful Schools for Young Adolescents. New Brunswick, N.J.: Transaction, 1984. 223 pp. $9.95; available from the Center for Early Adolescence, The University of North Carolina-Chapel Hill, Suite 223, CarrMill Mall, Carrboro, NC 27510.

Studies That Focus on the Improvement Process

URBAN EDUCATION STUDIES, directed by Francis S. Chase for the Council of the Great City Schools. The purpose of the project was to identify "strategies and developments which seem likely to contribute to the revitalization of educational institutions, personnel, and practices" in large urban schools. To this end, this project gathered information on programs in 16 large school districts, with special attention given to conditions offering promise of system-wide improvement. Data gathering included extensive survey research as well as on-site visits.

The project was primarily interested in educational innovation and revitalization at the school-system level. It found that such revitalization must include at least the following elements:

● Efforts to ensure that the basic skills for learning are acquired by every child in the primary school and strengthened in subsequent years.

● Curriculum adapted to the cultures, native languages, special talents, handicaps, preferred learning styles, and aspirations of individuals.

● Valuing everyone for whom the school system is responsible: both staff and students. This means there is a continuing search for developable capabilities and talents, high performance expectations, and recognition and reinforcement of worthy aspirations.

● Optional settings for learning designed so that students and their parents may select institutions fitted to their needs and aspirations.

● Coordination of in-school and out-of-school experiences by treating parents as partners in education.

● Effort to enlist the support of a wide variety of community enterprises and agencies so that education may be enhanced by the resources and opportunities.

● Effective provision for continuing education of all school system personnel.

● Systems of planning, management, and evaluation that permit effective use of resources.

* * * * *

Chase, Francis et al. Educational Quandaries and Opportunities. Washington, D.C.: Council of the Great City Schools, 1980. 188 pp.

Chase, Francis. Cross-District Analysis of Issues and Facts Associated with System-Wide Improvement in City Public Schools. Washington, D.C.: Council of the Great City Schools, 1980. 88 pp.

The Council of the Great City Schools, 1413 K Street NW, Washington, DC 20005

REDEFINING GENERAL EDUCATION IN THE AMERICAN HIGH SCHOOL, a project of the Association for Supervision and Curriculum Development (ASCD), directed by Dr. Gordon Cawelti. This project organized a network of 17 high schools, each of which attempted to formulate "a curriculum design that will better prepare students for the future." Each school examined its own programs and redesigned a general education curriculum. The project resulted in a model of a process for any school wishing to reform its general education program:

● Make a public commitment to rethink the school's general studies curriculum and set up the machinery to do so.

● Choose a conception of general education.

● Define the elements to be included in the education of each student, based upon the concept developed.

● Develop a new curriculum around the specific elements defined.

● Recommend that the local board of education adapt the new course requirements and other elements recommended for the new curriculum.

• Implement the new curriculum through material selection and staff development, and plan for an assessment of learning.

Central to the project is a belief that greater commitment to change comes when schools and communities join in this kind of analysis and curriculum design. Although each network school came to its own conclusions on general education and specific curricula, some common elements emerged. All schools increased the number of units required for graduation; most increased the requirements in science and mathematics; several instituted an arts requirement; and all reduced the time for elective courses.

ASCD hopes to develop regional networks that continue this process in high schools throughout the country. As an initial effort, ASCD brought together 22 high schools in a two-year High School Future Planning Network.

The network's activities will include analysis of current reform proposals, as well as examination of changing life styles, development of strategic planning skills, consideration of new forms of technology, and such curriculum issues as what "global interdependency" really means for instruction. The participating schools are also expected to study the implications of changing occupational trends on the curriculum. (ASCD Update, February 1984, p. 7)

* * * * *

ASCD Curriculum Update (Quarterly)

A book documenting the experiences and conclusions of the initial phase of this project will be available during the summer of 1984.

The Association for Supervision and Curriculum Development, 225 North Washington Street, Alexandria, VA 22314

THE SCHOOL IMPROVEMENT PROJECT, developed by the Institute for the Development of Educational Activities (I/D/E/A) and directed by Gilbert Johnson and Gary

Phillips. The project developed a process of school improvement, as follows:

● The school improvement effort must take place at the level of the individual school.

● The governance of the schools must include all those who are affected by decisions.

● The energy and the unique culture of the school must be used in its improvement; community leaders, parents, students, and professional educators must be included in both design and implementation.

● Improving the personal lives of individuals through planned, purposeful designs must be considered.

● The role of the external agency is to build the capacity of the participants.

● Improvement is primarily a process, not a prescription; any process must include ways of securing support of participants and adjust new or organizational structures to encourage program's improvement.

This process includes four stages:

● Awareness and Strategic Planning: A team of educators, parents, and community leaders defines a "vision of excellence" for the school.

● Design: The team selects practices and programs to reach this vision.

● Implementation: These practices and programs are adopted by the school.

● Insuring Continuous Improvement: Institutionalization of these practices and programs, as well as of the school improvement process.

I/D/E/A reports that the School Improvement Project has been implemented in a number of secondary schools and has resulted in improved academic achievement; improved attendance; increased participation in extracurricular ac-

163

tivities; improvement in behavior; a decrease in disciplinary problems (which itself decreases the number of
suspensions and expulsions); a reduction in the dropout
rate among students; a reduction in staff absenteeism; a
decrease in vandalism; an increase in the number of elective courses students take; and increased participation
by parents and community groups.

* * * * *

Phillips, Gary L. A Successful Building-Based Approach to
School Improvement in a U.S. Urban High School.
Indianapolis: Butler University, 1983.

The I/D/E/A Reporter.   Dayton, Ohio: I/D/E/A, Spring
1983.

Pamphlets and informational brochures are available from:

Gilbert Johnson, I/D/E/A, P.O. Box 346, Wright Brothers
Branch, Dayton, OH 45409; or Gary Phillips, Butler
Leadership Center, I/D/E/A School Improvement Project,
Butler University, Robertson Hall — Room 219, 4600 Sunset
Avenue, Indianapolis, IN 46208

THE WISCONSIN PROGRAM FOR THE RENEWAL AND IMPROVEMENT OF
SECONDARY EDUCATION (WRISE), directed by Herbert J.
Klausmeier at the Wisconsin Center for Education
Research. Its purpose is to enable middle, junior, and
senior high schools to develop an internal capability for
continual educational improvement.

According to WRISE, a school that has developed an improvement capability annually identifies areas of needed
improvement, develops related improvement plans that involve measurable goals, implements the plans, monitors
programs, and evaluates goal attainment. WRISE dscribes
itself as not being a prescriptive program, but rather
the schools it works with select their own areas of
improvement.

Based upon cooperative research with secondary schools,
WRISE recommends three strategies as well as organiza-

tional structures and school processes to facilitate
implementation of the strategies, as follows:

● "Individual Education Programming Strategy: An
educational program of course work and other educational
activities is arranged for each student each semester
that satisfies the student's developmental characteristics and that also meets district and state requirements.
The advisor involves the student and the parents in
planning and evaluating the student's program."

● "Individual Instructional Programming Strategy: The
teacher in each of his or her classes arranges an instructional program suited to each student's educational
needs.   The amount of student-initiated and teacher-
directed individual, pair, small-group, and large-group
activity, as well as other teaching methods and use of
materials, [is] varied to take into account differences
among the students in entering achievement level,
learning styles, motivation, and other characteristics."

● "Goal-Setting Strategy: The school's improvement
committee, with input from the relevant staff, sets goals
annually for improving outcomes for a group of students,
e.g., Grade 7 attitudes toward school, Grade 9 math
achievement, Grade 12 attendance.   The committee monitors
and evaluates attainment of the goals."

The WRISE organizational structures and processes that
facilitate implementation of the improvement strategies
are as follows:

● "An Educational Improvement committee consisting of
the principal, a counselor, and representative teachers
is established to take initiative for identifying areas
of improvement each year and for implementing the improvement strategies."

● "The instructional staff and students are organized
into small groups for instruction."

● "Educational advising is personalized by having
teachers serve as educational advisors."

● "A curriculum is provided that is structured but that can be adapted to take into account the differing educational needs of students."

● "Student input regarding their own educational and instructional programs is arranged."

● "Test results and other evaluation information are used to improve student learning and teaching."

● "Parental and community input regarding curriculum, instruction, evaluation, and other matters is arranged."

● "Class schedules are arranged to permit groups of teachers with mutual interests to have a common planning period during the school day."

● "Inservice activities are conducted systematically and in a variety of ways, but especially during the teachers' common planning period."

● "District officials work with the school in planning the improvement program and district support is provided for it."

WRISE is being implemented, in part or totally, in at least 100 middle and junior high schools and 25 high schools. It has been evaluated by the Center, which ascertained that "concurrent implementation of the improvement strategies yielded substantially higher student achievement. Student attitudes toward schooling and average daily attendance increased or remained stable. A school that makes progress annually toward attaining desired student outcomes by implementing the improvement strategies is regarded as having developed its own improvement capability."

The Department of Public Instruction of Wisconsin endorsed the program in 1982, and a WRISE consortium consisting of seven state universities and regional Cooperative Education Service agencies started implementing the program throughout Wisconsin in 1983.

WRISE materials include a volume explaining the improvement strategies and organizational structures, a second-

ary school improvement manual, and a series of audio-
visual materials that depict exemplary educational practices in a number of secondary schools. WRISE can be
used in a secondary school to initiate and maintain a
school improvement program.

* * * * *

For more information on the WRISE program and material,
contact the Wisconsin Center for Education Research, 1025
West Johnson Street, Room 796, Madison, WI 53706.

CITY HIGH SCHOOLS: A RECOGNITION OF PROGRESS, the 1984
report of a two-year project, the Ford Foundation City
High School Recognition Program, in which the Ford Foundation set out to identify, document, and recognize a
sample of urban high schools that had recently made significant gains. The Foundation undertook this project
because of its impression that, while public concern
about education was rising, the problems faced by the
most besieged part of the educational system--urban high
schools--had "bottomed out" and many of these schools
were on the road to recovery.

The project worked with cities to identify qualified
schools, issued nomination invitations to schools, and
followed up with site visits to nominated schools. The
purposes of the project were to build support for urban
schools, to find out whether some urban high schools were
indeed beginning to recover, and, if so, to explore the
factors that give a school the capacity for self-improvement.

Site visitors to the schools found instances of strong
improvement. Many of the schools were now:

● Experiencing social harmony after a long period of
tension.

● Servicing a larger, more diverse population with
greater degress of equity.

167

● Being better managed by vigorous leadership of principals, teachers, and counselors.

● Eliciting parent and community support.

● Using funds more effectively.

● Putting to good use the assistance of volunteers, business, and community agencies.

● Benefiting from establishment of new learning programs.

Some problems still existed:

● Rundown physical facilities.

● Reduction of funds, especially federal funds for programs for disadvantaged, handicapped, immigrant, and non-English-speaking students.

● "The current emphasis on minimum basic skills, with mandated curricula and methods of teaching and testing, has narrowed the scope of education for some students. Often, too, these mandated programs underuse teachers' abilities and, worse, neglect the development of students' abilities to think, analyze, and inquire. In some schools, the basic skills `floor´ has become the `ceiling´ of achievement."

● High rates of student turnover and absenteeism.

● Insufficient support for teacher development on the job.

● The expectation that high schools should meet many needs of students well beyond those related to academic or institutional needs.

The project team identified the following as characteristics that give a school the capacity to initiate and sustain improvements:

● Clarity that the primary mission is "providing a basic substantive high school education to all students."

● "The vision and determination of persons--teachers, parents, principals--along with the availability of resources....In many ways, the two were inseparable, but the sequence of people first and then resource seemed essential."

● Faculty and other staff working together more like a team than as separate departments or services.

● Principals have ongoing training and development in instructional leadership.

● Sustained systematic inservice or staff development programs for teachers.

● Clear, simple standards and rules for students-- developed with student and parent participation--and applied consistently and fairly.

● Access to modest discretionary funds for planning and testing classroom- and school-based instructional initiatives.

● Districts that encourage and support school-based plans for improving instruction.

● Solid working relations with such groups as out-of-school volunteers, local business and industry for career training, colleges and universities for assistance to academically talented students, and social service agencies that help students "at risk."

* * * * *

City High Schools: A Recognition of Progress. New York: The Ford Foundation, 1984.

The Ford Foundation, P.O. Box 559, Naugatuck, CT 06770 (203-729-3100)

PLANNING FOR TOMORROW'S SCHOOLS: PROBLEMS AND SOLUTIONS, one of a series of "Critical Issues Reports" published by the American Association of School Administrators. This study arrived too late for us to review but is mentioned here because it offers a planning guide and much valuable planning information, including:

● Models of the general planning process.

● Background information on demographic trends, future job trends, politics of school finance, and acceptable contemporary plans for school buildings and renovations.

● Concrete suggestions for sharing services among districts, building public confidence in local schools, working with business and industry in adopt-a-school projects, fund raising, and improving the quality of the teaching staff (with an analysis of the Japanese industrial concept of the "quality circle").

● Directions for curriculum change and a model for planning the changes.

● Issues in the use of computer technology and tips on planning for their use.

* * * * *

Planning for Tomorrow's Schools: Problems and Solutions. Arlington, Va.: American Association of School Administrators, 1983. 80 pp. $11.95

The American Association of School Administrators, 1801 North Mure Street, Arlington, VA 22209

CHAPTER FOUR
A Summary of the Recommendations

> Ideas which may seem a radical departure from
> what currently exists can help expand our vision
> of what is possible.
>
> -- Mary Hatwood Futrell, President
>   National Education Association

What do the recommendations add up to? Is there a core
of agreement? Are there strong disagreements, polarized
positions? Or do the studies talk past each other, with
different emphases and topics? One cogent criticism made
of a number of the studies is that their value is limited
because they do not systematically evaluate the cost and
benefits of proposals and alternatives. This is a valid
criticism, but perhaps educational cause and effect is
beset by too many variables for such analyses to be
worthwhile--it may be possible to estimate the costs but
not the outcomes. The most honest contribution may be to
suggest directions for improvement, and that is what the
studies do.

We believe that these studies do offer directions for
improvement and a collection of good ideas, based on at
least a core of agreement about the changes that need to
be made in education.

We have organized the recommendations into 11 major
areas, often pooling concrete recommendations from several studies where there seems to be an agreement on the
general direction for improvement. Any areas of disagreement, or topics clearly unaddressed, are pointed out.

What Should Be Taught

Different studies address this question in different
terms: goals, skills, values, understandings, descriptions of course contents, subject areas with number of
years recommended. However, there seems to be general
consensus that there should be a core curriculum for all
students, in which "higher-order" skills are given high

171

priority, and in which rigorous standards obtain, although they may be met in different ways by different students.

The core curriculum is to be designed so that it is:

- Organized by memorable themes and concepts, by methods of inquiry that cross disciplines, and by regular provisions for imparting knowledge, skills, and understandings.

- Sequenced so that levels of difficulty or complexity build on what was learned earlier.

- Uncluttered with electives or extraneous facts so students have opportunities to reapply and strengthen skills or to explore an issue or examine a work in depth.

- Adaptable so that the specific content can be chosen for student interest, and pace can be set for individual student needs without resorting to separate tracks.

All studies agree that the skills involved, the methods of inquiry, and the sense of intellectual purpose are more important than particular topics. In some studies, however (Mortimer Adler and the Paideia Group in The Paideia Proposal, and especially in Ernest L. Boyer's High School), certain works, issues, and human experiences are critically important as content for passing along a cultural heritage, and certain concepts are important for passing along a scientific and technological heritage.

The higher-order skills include those involved in analysis and interpretation of reading, defining a position in writing, inquiry, reasoning, and problem solving. Some studies hypothesize that concentration on basic skills, such as grammar, albeit needed and effective, has crowded out the teaching of higher-order skills. The recommendation is not to drop basic skills but to incorporate higher-order skills earlier.

The rigorous standards are the least well described of the recommendations. Although most reports recommend them, none specifies what "rigorous" means in any particular subject area. From the many recommendations for less passive and more open evaluation approaches, epitomized by the suggestion of "exhibitions" by Theodore R. Sizer in Horace's Compromise, it is clear that although the standards are to be rigorous, there should be a range of options in ways for students to show mastery.

Studies warn that higher standards should not be used to deny opportunities to minorities or disadvantaged students, but how to advance simultaneously toward the two goals of quality and equal opportunity is one of the most serious educational policy dilemmas of our time. The studies do not solve this dilemma. Harold Howe II, Senior Lecturer, Harvard Graduate School of Education, and former U.S. Commissioner of Education, warned in a speech to the Education Writers Association that more rigorous standards can simply work to increase the number of "dropouts" and "force-outs":

> Indeed, a school can make its average test score look really good by discouraging the kids with learning problems and getting them to drop out before they are required to take whatever tests are offered in senior year.

What should be taught in each subject area? Many studies recommend that certain skills should be taught in every appropriate area. These skills are: reading, with emphasis on inferential as well as literal comprehension; writing to promote analytic, interpretative, and evaluative skills; observing; describing; summarizing; inquiry; problem solving; application; creative thinking. Understanding, valuing, and judging should be taught as well, and these skills involve learning to ask a full range of questions on an issue. Finally, every area provides an opportunity to teach study skills, such as note taking.

• English and Communication Skills: Many reports select English literacy as the most important goal, to be attained through four years of study for all students.

In addition, Boyer's study recommends:

- A pre-high-school competency test and a summer remedial program, if indicated. Remedial help available as long as needed.

173

- A "basic English" course the first year, limited to 20 students, with plenty of opportunity for writing, teacher feedback, and rewriting.

- A study of key works from early Greek literature to the present, exploring common human dilemmas.

- Training in listening and speaking skills.

- Intensive work in critical reading and analytic writing.

- "Literacy" training in television, newspapers, and other forms of modern communication--"critical viewing, listening and reading." (The broadening of the domain of "communication" is reflected in Sizer's decision to discard the category of "English" and distribute what is usually taught under that name into two areas he calls "inquiry and expression" and "literature and the arts.")

● Mathematics: Most studies agree upon three years for all students, and four years for students who will major in math or science in college. One study recommends instead a two-year sequence for non-science majors. Another recommends the development of a new, demanding curriculum for non-college-bound students.

Whatever the course format, the National Science Board Commission on Precollege Education in Mathematics, Science and Technology report, Educating Americans for the 21st Century, recommends that the traditional content and approaches of the curriculum in algebra, geometry, pre-calculus, and trigonometry be reexamined and updated by:

- Using new computer technology and emphasizing algorithmic thinking for problem solving:

> Much of high school algebra consists of systematic methods for handling certain problems, e.g., factoring polynomials. Such methods are algorithms. Instead of making the student carry out such methods with paper and pencil a boring number of times, have the student do it just a few times and then program a computer to do it. The understanding gained should be at least as great. (Source Materials, p. 10)

174

- Student data gathering and exploring mathematical ideas to facilitate learning mathematics by discovery.

- Streamlining the traditional curriculum: for example, integrating aspects of geometry with other courses rather than isolating geometry in a year-long course.

- Adding important new topics such as discrete mathematics, elementary statistics, and probability.

Other studies support these additions and suggest as additional important topics: introduction to computers, and skills such as problem solving, application of math to problems of daily life, measurement, estimation, approximation, and testing the reasonableness of a solution.

● Science: Most studies with specific recommendations in this area recommend at least three years of high school science. The Educational EQuality Project of the College Board recommends that college applicants should also have a specialized knowledge in at least one area of science, either one of the traditional scientific disciplines or one of the newer, interdisciplinary fields. Ernest Boyer suggests a two-year program encompassing both the biological and physical sciences.

Educating Americans for the 21st Century recommends that the number of topics covered by science courses be drastically reduced and integrated around concepts and principles. This report and others recommend connectedness among the sciences, the introduction of teaching about technology into all science courses, and opportunities for students to practice skills such as observation, data collection, analysis, critical thinking, sequencing, making comparisons, and differentiating between fact and opinion and between inference and observation.

● Technology: Educating Americans for the 21st Century recommends that technology and engineering concepts be made part of the curriculum, not by creating separate courses but by introducing them into science and social studies courses. A list of proposed technology concepts and topics is included in the chapter three summary of the report.

● Computer Science: One-half semester is usually the length of time recommended for introductory computer study.

Some studies address computers in the math-science area and emphasize "hands on" experience and knowing how to use a computer. Others address computers in history of technology, claiming that the most important concepts to learn are when to use them, their strengths and limitations, and ethical issues. Some claim that understanding of computers can be best achieved by learning about their use through application activities in all areas of study.

Computers are also recommended as teaching tools that can be particularly helpful for individualizing instruction; this use will be discussed further under "Teaching Methods."

● Social Studies: Most studies recommend a three-year sequence including at least history, civics, and social science.

The following recommendations, pooled from Boyer, the Paideia Group, and Sizer, indicate that the social studies should include:

History, for knowledge about the development of institutions and ideas in the ancient and contemporary world, always including American history (approached through biographies of communities or individuals) and a study of non-Western history (approached through the in-depth study of one society). Geography should be included.

Civics, for an understanding of how our political institutions work--a study of American government (approached through exploration of one current controversial issue) and, perhaps, comparative government. Between civics and history, students should learn how a democratic society operates, the concepts of representative government and of conflict resolution through law--the difference between free and repressive societies.

History of technology, for a framework for the contemporary ethical and social issues surrounding the use of technology.

176

Ethical philosophy, because its focus on moral issues is very appealing to teenagers; it can be used within history courses to enhance interest.

Social science, at least one semester to familiarize students with social science methodology.

Skills, especially those for which social studies offers a particularly good context, and these are: the development and testing of hypotheses, analysis and evaluation of data, use of many forms of data, identifying the thesis in an argument, exploring historical cause and effect.

Values, judgments, and understandings can be fruitfully developed in social studies, using Socratic questioning to raise a range of key issues. A goal recommended by many studies is to develop an appreciation of diversity, to help students see that there may be numerous right answers to any situation that human societies face, but to see, as well, that some answers are definitely wrong. (This goal is deemed important because developmentally teenagers emerge from childhood's all-right or all-wrong perceptions to the other extreme of total relativity and "what feels right is right.") These goals may be difficult to implement, however, because even a narrow range of relativity is not comfortable for some parents, and there may be no community consensus on "the definitely wrong answer."

Economics is recommended by two other studies. The Education Commission of the States (ECS), in Action for Excellence, suggests as two economic competencies, "the ability to understand personal economics and its relationship to skills required for employment" and the "ability to understand our basic economic system (e.g., profit, revenues, basic law of supply and demand, etc.)." Princeton: A Place for Learning recommends that all students learn about the structure of a modern economy with its systems of banking, investment, credit, and money.

● Foreign Language: Most studies suggest a minimum of two years, following a foundation of several years in elementary school, with three years for students who will go on to college study in relevant fields. The goals for most studies are proficiency in speaking and the understanding of another culture. In A Place Called School, John I. Goodlad emphasizes, instead, the goal of better understanding of language and skill in language arts.

Sizer, noting that one goal for foreign language study is often to lessen ethnocentrism, suggests that social studies is a better area for accomplishing this goal. He does not recommend foreign language study for students still struggling to master their own language unless they will have an immediate opportunity to use the language.

● Health: Only Boyer makes an explicit recommendation for a one-semester health course, and he recommends that the content be the human body, what contributes to health, and how health affects other aspects of living. The teacher should be specifically qualified in health education. Sizer acknowledges the importance of health education and suggests that it be taught in the science area.

● The Arts: A good number of studies, including those that are most intent on streamlining the curriculum, recommend that study of the arts be a required part of the curriculum, with students having in-depth experience with at least one of the arts.

The studies generally recommend that art courses aim not at performance goals but rather at:

- Extending the range of means of expression.

- Using art as a key to understanding other cultures.

- Developing the type of creative thinking that will be needed in rapidly changing, technological times.

- Developing appreciation, which can be a great source of satisfaction in life.

● Preparation for Work: Many studies affirm the importance of helping students with the transition to work or further study. Few recent studies see the present form of vocational education that prepares students for specific jobs as effective for this goal. The arguments are that vocational education in its present form is obsolete because it uses out-of-date equipment, trains students for dead-end jobs, does not train them in general work skills or learning how to learn so that they have job mobility, and, in fact, cannot possibly train students for the full array of changing jobs in the modern world. Moreover, minorities and disadvantaged students are disproportionately assigned to vocational education, and since it is all but impossible to transfer into an academic track, this assignment means a permanent cutting off of options.

Several of the recent studies recommend an end to vocational education; those that do not, urge vocational education departments to create partnerships with businesses to acquire up-to-date information for course content, better equipment for training, and job-site learning opportunities. The Walls Within, the study of the Experience-Based Career Education program, suggests, however, that it may be difficult to achieve all that is hoped for from school-business partnerships. It is important to mention that while many of the current studies are critical of the content and philosophy of vocational education, the same studies praise the methods of vocational education teachers and the relationships these teachers are able to establish with students.

Beyond vocational education for specific jobs, and beyond career days, many studies recommend a one-half-semester "Introduction to the World of Work," and/or electives selected toward that goal. The course would explore attitudes about work over time and cultures, examine factors that determine the rewards for different types of work, and study a particular industry in depth.

● Electives and Student Choice: "Too many!" is the judgment of almost all of the recent studies. Apparently, electives make up 50% of the program for many students. The proposals for cutting down electives range in severity: the Paideia Group rules out any electives except for the choice among foreign languages; Sizer recommends that students be encouraged to pursue content that interests them but maintains that since the whole curriculum should be individualized these choices can be accommodated within the four areas he prescribes. Goodlad reserves 10% of

179

a student learning program for individual choice that would allow the student to develop and refine an area of individual interest and talent development. He suggests a voucher system through which students could participate in outside classes or private tutelage for this portion of their education and thus not be limited to what happens to be available in their school. Boyer recommends cutting the time devoted to electives to a maximum of one-third; his proposed one semester of independent study is another opportunity for personal choice, albeit academic choice. Willard Wirtz, in On Further Examination, recommends against a radical cutting of electives that are designed to motivate non-college-bound students and may actually be the more useful courses for them. Mary Anne Raywid, in The Current Status of Schools of Choice in Public Secondary Education, makes it clear that room for choice is important in motivating students, especially high-risk students, but she also stresses the importance of coherence and organizing principles in a curriculum. In general, the studies see electives as opportunities for students to gain experience and knowledge that will inform future choices, but recommend that they be carefully chosen and have a well-defined purpose.

● Service: Boyer recommends that the high school curriculum add a new "Carnegie Unit": a half-semester of service to community or school, with the administration of the service unit to be the responsibility of students.

● Extracurricular Activities: While some studies acknowledge that extracurricular activities (such as newspaper and debating) provide good educational opportunities, these studies and others note the problem that in large schools usually only the most confident students become involved, while nonparticipants are those who would benefit most. The implication is that at present extracurricular activities do not represent a good use of school resources. Either broader participation should be encouraged (and perhaps monitored by guidance counselors) or fewer resources should be devoted to the activities.

Joan Lipsitz, however, in Successful Schools for Young Adolescents, takes a very positive view, describing successful schools in which extracurricular activities are a key element in self-esteem and motivation. These schools

180

set a priority on providing many routes for rewards: intramural teams, outings, community service projects, arts and crafts; they can apparently be a strong influence in reducing anonymity and "binding students to the school culture."

It is not clear whether, if given unlimited resources, most researchers would support extracurricular activities with broadened participation, or would wish to cut them in any case to give the message that school is for the cultivation of intellect.

● Physical Education: Goodlad's study favors keeping physical education as part of the regular curriculum and recommends that it prepare students for sports they can play as adults when they will not have access to team sports.

Sizer, in contrast, recommends that physical education be an extracurricular activity and that the health education normally taught as part of physical education become part of the math/science program.

* * * * *

The foregoing are the elements of the curriculum discussed by the recent studies. There is some agreement on major issues. The studies agree on the need for a streamlined core curriculum to be taken by all students, with a higher-order skills orientation, and rigorous standards (that some studies recommend be met in individualized ways and that are not to be used to penalize minority or disadvantaged students). Whether this last part of the recommendation can be implemented effectively is questionable. There is substantial agreement on what the major elements of the curriculum should be. No one is suggesting departures in opposite directions, such as teaching of more factual content.

There is disagreement on the permissibility of electives, with the Paideia Group allowing none, but, as Sizer points out, such a program can accommodate some range of individual students' interests. All studies agree on the direction of cutting down. How much room there would truly be for individual choice and pace in a program such as Paideia remains to be seen: the Paideia Group's forthcoming third volume may be informative on this issue.

Is there disagreement with the "back to basics" movement, which does not seem to have much of a voice in the current studies? The word "basic" is used in at least two ways in debates on education. In "basic skills" it is used to mean elementary, those skills that build the foundation for others. There is probably agreement as to what they are—decoding skills in reading, grammar and punctuation in writing, computational skills in math; in this meaning of "basics," no one is suggesting neglecting them but rather phasing in the higher-order skills earlier. The second use of "basic" refers to the most important elements and this aim is somewhat reflected in general recommendations to streamline the curriculum.

Although many specifics are recommended for curriculum content, the following statement in <u>Princeton: A Place for Learning</u> best captures the sense of recommendations for what should be taught.

> Beyond the basic disciplines, what subjects are taught is less important than how they are taught and the ends to which they are taught. There are many ways of exploring heritage, as there are various approaches to uncovering the workings of society or of scouting the domain of experience and learning. When an educational program is guided by a concept of functional literacy, integration rather than coverage becomes the measure of comprehensiveness. Decisions concerning the curriculum should derive from a sense of the overall goals of the program and of the integration needed to achieve them. The methods of teaching, the processes of administration, and the interaction of everyone in the system should reflect the respect for persons, ideas, and inquiry that we believe is at the base of our educational goals. (p. 28)

There is disagreement on the goals of teaching about computers, some believing that the main focus should be on the "why's" and social issues of computer use, others believing the focus should be on developing computer use skill by hands-on activities. All, however, believe that students' familiarity with computers should be increased.

182

There seems to be general agreement with the direction of recommendations surrounding vocational education—that it should be greatly improved or that it should be phased out—but there are other views not reflected in these studies.

We have two questions about the recommendations of the set of studies. The first is about an area we find missing. Consider the Paideia Group's statement of the main objectives of education:

> ...these three objectives are determined by the vocations or callings common to all children when they grow up [a] as citizens, [b] earning their living, and [c] putting their free time to good use. (p. 16)

These "callings" leave out the important one of raising a family, and none of the proposals that specify curriculum content suggests education for that role. Courses in marriage and in family dynamics are often the first to be cut as "frills," and while we are not judging the quality of existing courses, we believe that learning how to raise a family is surely one of the "basics" and merits educational attention. If a more direct link to education is needed to persuade educators that family life and childrearing are worthwhile school subjects, consider how often the "condition of the family" is blamed for today's education problems. Then consider the impact on education of assuring that the next generation of children has parents who have been educated in nutrition, child development, ways to resolve family problems, and ways to stimulate children's interest and respond to their learning needs.

The second question is about a discrepancy between the issues-oriented approach to curriculum being proposed and the fact-oriented testing of some college admission examinations. One top-rated public high school, in fact, advises its students not to take the achievement tests in American history, because the school's issue-oriented curriculum puts them at a disadvantage. The College Board's Educational EQuality Project stresses the importance of skills, and many other studies address the difficulty of teaching higher-order skills in a fact-laden context. The Educational EQuality Project report does

183

not provide guidance on the issue of whether college admission testing may move in a direction more consonant with what is being recommended by the studies.

As a final comment on what should be taught, we wish to acknowledge the difficulty of creating and implementing a core curriculum for all, given the great heterogeneity of the American population. Although we support the goal that the curriculum be adaptable to many variables, we know that this goal only adds to the difficulty of the task.

Teaching Methods

Recommendations for improving teaching methods fall into six categories: time-on-task; individualizing of teaching, with special emphasis on the use of coaching to teach skills; better remediation; variety in techniques, particularly the use of techniques that encourage active student participation; use of Socratic discussion to develop understandings; and use of techniques that foster academic self-esteem. Some of these categories overlap (e.g., coaching involves active student participation), but we will go through the categories one by one, discussing the rationales and the specific suggestions offered by the studies.

• Time-on-Task: An almost universal complaint concerning high school education is the amount of time spent in activities other than teaching and learning. Creating Effective Schools, a program for school improvement developed by supporters of the Effective Schools Movement, maintains that "time-on-task" is probably the most significant factor affecting student achievement. The reports offer several policy options to increase students' time-on-task, and while most relate to school organization and scheduling, some concern teaching methods. A Nation at Risk, the report of the National Commission on Excellence in Education, recommends expanding the time available for learning through better classroom management. The Education Commission of the States recommends both an increase in homework and application of techniques (such as those developed by the Effective Schools Movement) that increase time-on-task in

184

the classroom. Some of these techniques are described in ECS publications as follows:

- Focus teaching and curriculum selection on the basic skills or agreed-upon academic focus of the school, maintain a fast pace, and cover content extensively.

- Maintain a high student success rate, especially for the introduction of new content, seatwork, and homework. Challenging students with difficult work for which the success rate is low generally is not effective.

- Monitor individual student performance, praise correct answers, and provide individual, specific, academically oriented corrective feedback on incorrect answers.

- Have a well-organized classroom that includes training students in classroom procedures and transition processes (especially at the beginning of the school year), and a clear, fair, and uniform disciplinary system.

● Individualization: Many of the recommended improvements in teaching methods have individualization at their heart. More individualization is, in fact, one of the strongest recommendations that emerges from the studies. Individualization refers both to one-to-one teaching techniques and to the development of teacher-student relationships that have some continuity. Individualization is recommended most frequently in response to student problems with learning skills (especially higher-order skills), but it is also recommended to counter motivational problems and to prevent or manage discipline problems. These recommendations are based on the assumption that, in general, the better a teacher knows a student, the more likely the teacher is to be able to diagnose, anticipate, and respond to learning problems, find ways to motivate the student, and prevent behavior problems, and the more likely the student is to want to perform well and behave well for the teacher. Goodlad refers to a study that affirms the educational importance of teacher-student relationships.

Flanagan interviewed intensively a sample of 1000 adults, aged 30....There is little in the data to suggest that the high school curriculum contributed to

185

job competence or satisfaction, later participation in civic and political activities, or life enjoyment. What these young adults remembered about schools were the learnings that creative teachers had managed to link up with their lives at the time they were adolescents. (pp. 14-15)

Several studies make a strong case for the use of individual coaching, or coaching in small groups, to develop intellectual skills, using a model from athletic training to make a point about academic training: that skills cannot be taught by lecturing, because a teacher has to have the student's behavior to work with. A student has to perform, a teacher has to give specific feedback, the student perform again, the teacher evaluate again, and the cycle repeated several times. A teacher who believes that a student is not making progress with a specific method can suggest an alternative appropriate to the student's particular difficulty; if the student is working intuitively and headed in an unproductive direction, the teacher can redirect the thinking process with questions. The environment for coaching, one study cautions, must be one in which it is safe to make mistakes (where students can, in fact, examine their own mistakes to further their learning) and where attention focuses on the thinking process rather than the answer.

As with coaching, many of the other improvements in method recommended for teaching higher-order skills have as a central goal that teachers be able to examine and work with an individual student's thinking process. For example, virtually all of the studies recommend that students be asked to write more in every subject area (and in math to show problem-solving ability in a stepwise fashion), because writing helps students clarify their thinking and gives both student and teacher an opportunity to analyze and redirect the thinking process. The studies emphasize that student writing must be corrected promptly, with enough specificity to be helpful. Many studies recommend greatly curtailing the use of multiple choice, true/false, and short-answer tests, claiming that they are unproductive for teaching higher-order skills because they encourage students to focus on unconnected bits of information and because they do not give teachers much information about individual students' thinking processes.

186

One study points out that individualization gives an important message in personalizing instruction: a teacher's finding the right pace or method for a student not only helps a student learn a particular skill, but it also conveys that the student is important.

Another study makes the point that teachers must know students well enough to know about problems in subject areas other than their own because a skill deficiency in one area may affect others.

The studies present many and varied supporting arguments for increasing individualization. All studies that address teacher-student relationships maintain that continuity in such relationships is important and beneficial, and we see yet another reason to support it. One criticism of the studies as a whole is that they do not offer recommendations for character development. We believe that the recommended continuity in teacher-student relationships is a strong support to character development, whether or not the recommendations had this as an explicit aim.

With respect to classroom teaching, the one major dissent on individualization is to be found in Creating Effective Schools, whose authors point out that "a national study of innovative instructional practices found no evidence that individualized instructional programs enhanced achievement." However, they do allow that personalized instruction should be used for "correction, enrichment, or extension learning" and "supplementing whole class instruction."

Other recommendations of the Effective Schools Movement (for example, that it is important to find the right level of challenge) seem to necessitate individualization or small-group work. Thus it is not clear how much this group differs from other current studies in its view of the right balance between individualized and whole-class instruction. Some of its literature, in fact, encourages small-group work, which can have some of the advantages of individual work (pacing adjusted to the students' needs) but can have new disadvantages (tracking and labeling within the class).

What guidance do the studies offer educators in implementing individualization? Two kinds of guidance are needed. One is administrative and concerns the development of school organization that fosters long-term teacher-student relationships, school scheduling that provides frequent opportunity for one-to-one work with students, and the reallocation of personnel and resources that make increased one-to-one work affordable. Even with the best reallocations, it is likely that schools will need substantially increased funding to provide the level of individualization recommended by the studies. The studies' recommendations on these issues will be discussed later under "School Organization."

The second kind of guidance concerns teacher education for the decisions and techniques involved in individualizing instruction and orchestrating the resulting classwork. Suggestions for orchestrating a number of different activities in a class are offered by the Wisconsin Program for the Renewal and Improvement of Secondary Education (WRISE) and the Effective Schools Movement (although their hearts may not be in individualization). Programs for understanding and responding to different learning styles (from a particular theoretical perspective) are presented in several individual papers in the University/Urban Schools National Task Force Conference proceedings. (Other papers in these reports are also interesting for skills teaching methods because they are concerned with the teaching of reasoning skills.) Coaching is described by the Paideia Group and illustrated by a number of examples given by Sizer.

As with other teaching techniques, however, individualization is as much an art as a science, and this dual nature needs to be reflected in the way teachers are educated. Individualization may become more of a science as we discover more about the learning process and individual variation, but, at present, apprenticeship with opportunity to observe skilled teachers at work and conferences where different approaches can be presented and compared will probably be the major sources of help for teachers. Both of these are recommended by the studies, as readers will see in the recommendations under "Teachers."

● Remediation: Many of the studies stress the importance of careful attention to remediation, recognizing
that students without adequate basic skills will have
continuing achievement problems. Interest in remediation
is an extension of the studies' interest in individuali-
zation--looking at the needs of individual students and
recognizing that not all students' needs can be met in
the same way. In fact, the Paideia Group and Sizer,
favoring essentially individual tracks for all students,
do not view remediation as a separate issue.

The studies approach remediation differently, some
focusing on when and where remediation needs should be
diagnosed and treated, others suggesting methods. None
outlines a comprehensive approach, but this was not any
of the studies' mission.

Most of the studies recommend standardized testing at
transitional points in schooling so that schools can give
remedial help at key times. Many studies take a firm
stand against social promotions, i.e., promoting students
who have not achieved the expected skills in order to
keep them with their peers. In the views of these
studies, at least some remediation should take place
during a repeated year within the normal classroom setting; some specify that diagnosis and extra remedial work
are essential, as well as holding a student back to
repeat the year. Goodlad cautions that having students
repeat a year rarely helps, because schools are not
likely to diagnose students' particular problems. Not
favoring the option of repeating a year, he recommends
that well-designed remedial work be given during the time
allocated to the subject area in question, and not be
given in the limited time his proposed program allocates
for individual choice. Boyer emphasizes the year before
high school as a time for assessing every student's
language proficiency, so that the summer can be used for
remediation. In addition, high school students who
continue to need remedial help should have it available
as long as needed, and all students should take a basic
English course to prepare for the reading and writing
requirements of a high school education. Such a course
would attend to the more limited "remedial" needs of a
great number of entering students.

189

As for methods for working with students with remedial needs, Raywid's study states the importance of establishing short-term, achievable subgoals, planning academic programs for early and frequent successes, and providing many opportunities for experiential learning. Specific suggestions on remediation methods are given by some of the reports in the University/Urban Schools Conference proceedings; one study presents a view of the basic component abilities needed for academic success, and another addresses recognizing and responding to different learning styles. There is, of course, a vast literature on remediation outside the scope of the current studies.

• <u>Variety in Teaching Techniques and Active Student Involvement</u>: The way most of the current observers characterize the average high school classroom is epitomized by Goodlad's description of a teacher-dominated classroom in which the teacher makes virtually all the decisions--from where the students will sit to what the learning goals will be. Goodlad reports that in such a classroom the teacher "out-talks" the class by a ratio of three to one. There is little variety in methods, and included are only those that require passive student behavior: listening to lectures and doing seatwork. The seatwork is even more passive than it need be: rather than writing out their ideas, students fill in the blanks in workbooks. Whether the problem comes from the student or from the school environment, this decade's main student problem, in contrast to that of previous decades, is reported to be passivity, not disruptiveness.

Many of the studies make a plea for more variety in teaching methods, and especially for opportunities for which students to take an active role in their own learning, both to make meaningful what they learn now and to help them learn how to be learners in the future. The studies recommend having students set their own goals for learning; adding to the lecture mode such learning activities as role playing, hands-on exercises, discussions with Socratic questioning, field trips, library research, individual coaching, peer teaching, having students take practice quizzes before the exams that count so that they can appraise and correct their own learning; and frequent rearrangement of classrooms to change groupings for different learning purposes.

190

Virtually all studies that address teaching methods support more variety in techniques and more active student
learning. None describe the techniques in any detail or
discuss the criteria in deciding which technique to use,
except for the formula presented by the Paideia Group and
Sizer of lecture for information, coaching for skills,
and Socratic discussion for values and understandings. A
number of studies, however (Sizer, Boyer, and Sara Lightfoot in The Good High School), give generative illustra-
tions of teachers involving students in active learning.

● Socratic Questioning to Develop Values and Understandings: This technique (in addition to individual
coaching, which was discussed earlier) is given enough
attention by several studies to merit separate discussion. In Socratic questioning the subject of discussion
is usually a values judgment--what is good, what is
right--and, as Sizer explains, the teacher asks questions
from a variety of viewpoints, and then, just when students are sure they have made the right decision, have
considered all factors, and have developed their rationale, the teacher will ask a question from another viewpoint, throwing new light on the discussion and un-
settling the earlier decision.

The rationale for the process seems to be based on the
concept that judgment or wisdom is a matter of knowing
the key questions to ask. Knowing the range of questions
to ask on an issue is, in turn, greatly aided by a
thinker's ability to consider an issue from a full range
of viewpoints. The teacher in Socratic questioning
actually gives students a model for their own thinking
and demonstrates both the process of questioning and the
type of factors and viewpoints that should be considered.

To carry out this technique in an educational way, a
teacher must be willing to have all sides of an issue
presented in class; in communities with a strong viewpoint on a particular topic, this can sometimes be a
controversial process.

The Paideia Group specifies that the conditions for such
discussions include having a group of between 20 and 25
students seated around a table, with the timing of the
discussion flexible so that the teacher can carry it on

191

long enough to bring it to a good close. Paideia recommends that if a school cannot implement the total Paideia proposal at one time, Socratic discussion is an important and feasible starting point.

● Fostering Academic Self-Esteem and Motivation: The problem of student passivity has led a number of studies to recommend techniques that foster academic self-esteem --the student's belief that he or she can succeed academically--and techniques that otherwise enhance academic motivation. Some of the already-mentioned recommendations for improved techniques are useful in achieving these goals as well as specific academic learning: for example, a classroom climate where mistakes are safe, a teacher's finding the right pace or method for a student, continuity in student-teacher relationships, small and attainable goals for a student's remedial needs.

Other recommendations for enhancing self-esteem and motivation are the elimination of tracking by academic ability (this issue will be discussed under "School Organization"), students and teachers working together on a project outside class (where a teacher can see abilities and interests that might not be apparent in class), and careful listening to students in class discussions. In contrast to the transitional nod that Goodlad describes as a common teacher response to student comments, Sizer describes a teacher who brings in each student's comment at the end of a discussion, showing that each student had something of value to contribute.

Media

The media discussed most frequently by the studies are books, computer-assisted instruction, and television and video tape.

There seems to be general agreement on two points related to the use of media by the schools. One is that the people directly in charge of its use for instruction (usually the teachers) should have the strongest voice in media selection. The second is that new technologies can be important in individualizing and varying instruction. There seems to be neither the untempered optimism nor the

fear that new technologies would replace teachers and
dehumanize instruction that were common in earlier
decades. A warning of several studies is that schools
should analyze why and how they will use new technologies
before purchasing. Points made by different studies are
presented below.

● Books: Many studies maintain that textbooks, especially those in math and science, need updating. Some
studies urge educators to rely less on textbooks, which
often present a single viewpoint and lack the excitement
of original research, and to rely more on primary source
materials. All studies that address the issue recommend
that there be less state control over book content and
that teachers have the main say in book selection. One
study recommends less district control and more teacher
control over purchasing practices; for example, a teacher
may find six copies of five different books more useful
than thirty copies of the same book. The studies do not
discuss the nongovernmental groups and individuals that
influence book selection, and thus they offer little help
to educators and school systems in dealing with local
citizen groups and national lobbying groups.

● Computer-Assisted Instruction: Many studies recommend
computer-assisted instruction to help individualize skill
practice with needed drills and remedial exercises in
areas from math and science to language learning. Educating Americans for the 21st Century suggests ways computers should be used to update mathematics and science
teaching, and the report provides some cautions, too.
Boyer suggests that schools be selective in the use of
computers for instruction, and that before they make
purchasing decisions they explore with computer firms the
resources the firms might offer the school--for example,
willingness to help teachers develop and publish software
for their own courses.

● Television, Video and Audio Tape: A number of studies
propose that these media be used to advantage to record
superior lectures and thus to extend students' exposure
to the arts, scientific experimentation, and other
experience that cannot be brought into the classroom.
This use of media is, the studies emphasize, not intended
to supplant feasible hands-on experience for students.

Studies recommend that at least one cable channel in a community be devoted to school use.

Evaluation and Guidance

The studies make recommendations on several aspects of the evaluation and guidance process, focusing on both the daily process of evaluating student work and the long-term process of evaluating and guiding a student.

- <u>Tests Used as Teaching Tools</u>: Tests are teaching tools because, in addition to their motivating effects, they tell students what aspects of a course to focus on, and they give students information about their own knowledge and skills. As noted earlier, the studies recommended much less dependence on multiple choice, true/false, and short-answer tests, and much greater use of essays. Essays emphasize developing a line of thought that <u>uses</u> information rather than simply reproducing it and provide a record of the thinking process for teachers and students to review.

- <u>More Individualized Testing</u>: In addition to recommending testing in the form of essays, which students can develop in a variety of directions depending on individual interest, Sizer recommends that the ultimate way of testing high school achievement and a student's readiness for graduation be a series of "exhibitions" in which students demonstrate that they have mastered the required course of study. Such exhibitions are to be scheduled individually, when students feel ready for them.

- <u>Standardized Testing at Transition Points</u>: <u>A Nation at Risk</u>, among other studies, recommends standardized tests at transition points to determine students' need for remediation. Boyer particularly emphasizes testing before high school entrance so that students can have intensive remediation the summer before entering.

- <u>Development of a Test to Guide All Students</u>: Boyer recommends the development of a test (he calls it the SAAT—Student Achievement and Advisement Test) that can be used for advising all students, both college- and non-college-bound, about their futures. This test would be one component of a more comprehensive student evaluation program that would also include such items as teacher evaluations and portfolios containing examples of students' work.

● Smaller Case Loads for Counselors: Boyer recommends a maximum of 100 students per guidance counselor.

● Monitoring of Extracurricular Participation: Goodlad points out that extracurricular activities can be key to a student's self-esteem but that only a small proportion of students in a large school participate. He suggests that guidance counselors note participation patterns and try to get more students involved. (There is an apparent contradiction between recommendations for cutting extracurricular activities and recommendations for broadening participation in them. The studies conclude that either option would be a better use of resources than the current situation, in which a broad range of extracurricular activities is participated in by the same few students.)

● Seeking Input from Industry for Better Vocational Guidance: Several studies recommend that counselors should seek consultation from industry to keep up with current job-market needs and the skills and characteristics sought in employees.

● Follow-Up Surveys of High School Graduates: Boyer maintains that high schools cannot assess their success without information on the fortunes of their graduates. Follow-up surveys could indicate to a school where it does and does not offer good preparation.

Special Student Populations

Many of the studies mention ways to meet the needs of particular types of students, but there seems to be no particular pattern to the recommendations except agreement that student needs that differ from those of the mainstream should be given attention. This is consistent with the general support of individualization. Some recommendations require considerable funding, and it is not clear what level of funding should be devoted to resources recommended for special populations when choices among priorities must be made. The following recommendations are pooled from the studies.

● Gifted Students: Several studies note that programs for these students need the most attention, since it is the performance of gifted students that has declined most in recent years. However, the Paideia Group maintains that no special resources are needed because its proposed program provides enough range of opportunity. A special track for each student should be developed by a group of "house teachers" (the group of teachers assigned to a small number of students in the proposed small-unit structures, or "houses," within schools).

Other recommendations for gifted students made by one or more of the studies are:

- The opportunity to "test out" of a regular course into a more advanced one.

- Special programs after regular school time.

- Special, sometimes residential, academies.

- Taking college courses while still a high school student.

- Early college entrance.

- Advanced classes in math/science, which should be offered by all schools.

● Students with Learning Problems in Any Subject: These students should be able to be accommodated in the normal course of activity in such proposals as Paideia's in that each student is to have an individual track developed by small group of house teachers. In addition:

- English language proficiency of all students should be assessed before high school, and a remedial summer course taken if needed.

- All students should be kept in same program, not tracked (this view is supported by most of the studies).

- Remedial help should be available in extra time after school, not in the limited time to be allowed for electives.

- Peers can provide help in class.

- Federal funds can be used to encourage creation of small, individualized programs for those with serious learning problems.

• Students Who Do Not Meet Minimum Standards in a Grade: These students should not be promoted for social reasons, according to A Nation at Risk and other studies. This recommendation runs counter to those of Goodlad and others that students should not be grouped in any way that relates to ability. These two contrasting points of view can be reconciled only by recommendations of Sizer and Paideia that an individual track be designed for each student.

• Minority and Disadvantaged Students: More rigorous standards should not be used to deny students educational opportunity. (As noted earlier, this recommendation is easier stated than implemented. Specific attention to policies and strategies is needed to make the statement more than rhetoric.)

Bilingual funds should be transferred to programs to help non-English-speaking students develop English literacy. (Literacy in English for all is the major goal of some of the studies. However, the majority of studies do not address bilingual education.)

Talent development among minority and female students should be emphasized.

• High-Risk Students: These students should be helped to establish attainable subgoals and to achieve success early and frequently. They should also have as an option alternative schools with much teacher-student contact and continuity. They could be affected adversely by other current recommendations, including more homework, more demanding courses, longer school hours, and more tests, which may, in fact, increase dropouts. As John Lawson, Massachusetts Commissioner of Education, is quoted as saying, "If a kid can't clear four feet, it doesn't do much good to raise the bar to four feet, six inches. It does help to give more and better coaching, more and better training."

● Dropouts: Community college programs should facilitate their return to education.

● Disruptive Students: The help recommended above for high-risk students should be available for disruptive students. If alternative schools fail to help, Sizer recommends that these students be expelled, with the same opportunity to return to education as is available for students who drop out.

School Organization and School Climate

It was noted under teaching methods that an almost universal complaint is the amount of time spent engaged in activities other than teaching and learning. A Nation at Risk and ECS make recommendations designed to increase time-on-task; some have to do with teaching methods and are presented in an earlier section. Those that concern school organization or climate are as follows:

● Time in School: A number of other studies support extending the school day or year, suggesting lengthening the school year to as much as 200 days from the current 180 days. However, some others, such as Boyer, maintain that "the urgent need is not lengthening the school day or school year, but in using more effectively the time schools already have," and thus recommend a class schedule that would allocate larger blocks of time to each class, which would promote a more in-depth instructional experience as well as reduce time wasted in changing classes and in "start-up" and "wind-down."

The time devoted to noninstructional matters, such as discipline, lunch, and changing classes, should be reduced. (For those who know the hectic pace of school lunch times, the recommendation that time for lunch be reduced can only convey the extremes to which concerned observers are willing to go to provide more education.)

198

• <u>Intrusions</u>: Administrative intrusions into instructional time should be reduced. The most common recommendation in the studies is to to do away with the public address system. Loudspeaker announcements and other forms of messages delivered in class time not only interrupt the learning process, the studies claim, but also give the message that serious intellectual work is not respected.

• <u>Discipline</u>: A clear disciplinary code should be fairly and consistently administered. This recommendation, offered by numerous studies, affirms those of earlier studies and is stated but not discussed in depth by current studies.

• <u>Academic Credit Requirements</u>: Academic credit required for graduation should be increased, and credit given for nonacademic experience (such as work) should be reduced. The first part of this ECS-offered recommendation runs counter to Sizer's plea (see below) for a reduction in the number of courses a student must take, unless more credit will be given per course (as might make sense if schools adopt Sizer's proposal to allocate more time for each course). The second part of this recommendation points in the opposite direction from Boyer's recommendation that a new Carnegie unit of credit be given for a semester of community service.

• <u>Scale and Structure</u>: One major theme in recommendations for changing school structure could be summarized as "small is beautiful": fewer students per teacher, fewer students and teachers per unit, fewer subject areas, fewer facts, fewer learning goals. The call for variety in teaching techniques, individualized teaching, and continuity in teacher-student relationships requires flexibility in use of time and space, and smaller school units. Sizer makes the point that both more scheduling flexibility and smaller units can be implemented with gains rather than losses for the entire school community, if schools adopt the view that "less can be more" when fewer subject areas and courses are offered with more time given to each. Sizer maintains that having each student take six or seven courses freezes the schedule, fragments the learning experience, and undermines the continuity of relationships. With fewer courses and more time, teachers can provide the kind of individualized programs that eliminate the need for putting students into separate academic tracks (see later recommendations on tracking). Thus, several recommendations dovetail.

Many studies recommend that large schools be organized into small units (one study suggests 150 students as the maximum size) with continuity over time in teacher and student groups, citing the following as the rationale for such organization:

- The feasibility of diagnosing learning problems and individualizing teaching is increased.

- Student-teacher relationships are a key factor in student motivation, and teacher motivation as well.

- Small units, by decreasing anonymity, are a preventive approach to discipline and to teacher burnout.

- The limited size of the teacher group increases the ease of arranging joint planning opportunities.

Sizer maintains that no teacher should teach more than 80 students, and that disciplinary specializations should be broken down, if necessary, to avoid exceeding this number (i.e., it is better for one teacher to teach 80 students both English and history than one teacher to teach 160 students English and another teacher teach 160 students history). In addition to the benefits that accrue to students from continuity in a relationship with a teacher, many studies maintain that teachers will also benefit because one key factor in burnout seems to be the number of barely known students teachers have to teach daily.

Decreasing the number of teachers any student will have is, of course, not without problems. Some provision must be made for the inevitable situations in which a student and a teacher do not get along in spite of efforts to make the relationship work. In this case, the intensity of more than one class together daily, or a student's having, say, mathematics mainly with one teacher year after year, could be as detrimental as it could be advantageous in the case of a good relationship. Another consideration is that of the "star" teacher whose class many students look forward to taking in junior or senior year; such an opportunity could be precluded by rigidly defined subunits. No doubt these are only two of many possible problems of reorganizing into smaller units.

Flexible time and space arrangements should allow teachers to make changes when needed (e.g., for an anticipated lengthy discussion class or a special coaching session). Sizer suggests that the only way to achieve such flexibility is to accept that "less can be more" and reduce the number of courses students are expected to take, consolidating learning goals within fewer courses.

● Other Recommendations: Other recommendations, some concerning school organization, some the school culture, and some both, aim ultimately to affect school and classroom climate in a way that will foster academic self-esteem on the part of all students:

Tracking by ability levels should be abolished, for the many reasons Goodlad presents: that students in lower tracks find lower expectations, poorer teaching, less emphasis on higher-order skills, and worse classroom climate, and that it is disproportionately minority and disadvantaged students who are assigned to the lower tracks—precisely those students who need better education opportunities. Instead, several studies suggest that teaching be individualized enough to allow teachers to establish a suitable program for any student within classes or mixed ability levels. Virtually all the studies that address tracking recommend abolishing it.

There should be many routes to rewards for students, and this means an expansion rather than a contraction of extracurricular activities. Lipsitz's studies suggest that providing opportunities beyond the usual few that engage a small core of students (e.g., interscholastic sports) increase motivation, decrease the sense of anonymity, and involve students in the school culture.

The school environment should be personalized into a community in which most teachers and students know each other well. By a "personalized" environment, studies seem to mean an environment that the students have had a hand in creating and that is warm and attractive. The

201

desirability of continuity in relationships and of avoiding a sense of anonymity has already been discussed.

A high level of academic expectations for students. This recommendation from earlier studies is reaffirmed and modified by current studies, which point out that the practice of tracking denies this expectation, but note that a school's level of expectations should be high enough to be challenging but not so high as to produce anxiety.

A climate where students are not afraid to make mistakes should not, in fact, be sabotaged by the high level of expectations. It should be an accepted attitude that mistakes give students opportunities to learn about their own learning process.

Teachers

In policy recommendations of the past decade, the principal has often been the star--the focus of strategies for change. In the current set of recommendations, with increased interest in student-teacher relationships and the individual student's learning process, the teacher is at front and center stage. The earlier view of the principal's role is not countermanded by current studies; these studies reaffirm the importance of the principal in establishing the general context for teaching activities, but the focus of new recommendations is the teacher.

The great majority of the studies deal with the role of the teacher and the conditions of teaching, and virtually all of these make recommendations for improving the situation that might be summarized.as a new "Three R's" for teachers: Room, Resources, and Respect. The recommendations are so numerous that they are dealt with only briefly in the following pages. Any one recommendation may have come from only one study, but all items are supported by a general sense of direction. There is only one area of explicit disagreement among the studies: whether or not the shortage in math and science teachers is best met by offering differentially higher pay for teachers in those fields. Educating Americans for the 21st Century is the only report to recommend differential pay; a number of other studies state that there should not be differential pay for different fields.

● Recruitment: Most studies recommend that efforts be made to recruit better candidates into teaching. These efforts include:

- Fiscal incentives, including scholarship aid and higher prospective salaries.

- Teacher cadet programs in high school.

- Special efforts to recruit high achievers into teaching.

● Training: The following excerpt from The Paideia Proposal conveys the tone of many of the current studies on the teaching task and the type of training and development it requires:

Teaching is one of the three great cooperative arts. The other two are farming and healing--the arts of agriculture and of medicine. All three are "cooperative" because they must work with nature to produce the goods they aim at.

The cooperative art of the farmer consists in making the best use of seed, soil, and weather to produce the livestock, grains, or fruits that nature is able to produce alone, without the farmer's help. The cooperative art of the physician consists in employing the body's own resources for healing--for maintaining or regaining health.

The cooperative art of the teacher depends on the teacher's understanding of how the mind learns by the exercise of its own powers, and on his or her use of this understanding to help the minds of others to learn.

Obviously, the future teacher's own experience in learning is indispensable to such an understanding. It is by the skillful use of this self-understanding that the teacher can help others to learn. This skillfulness is developed best by practice under supervision, that is, by coaching. All the skills of teaching are intellectual skills that can be developed only by coaching, not by lecture courses in pedagogy and teaching methods such as are now taught in most schools or departments of education and are now required for certification. (pp. 60-61)

Preservice training should include:

- A general college education.

- More education in subject matter than in educational techniques.

- Within the techniques, much more emphasis than at present on: teaching higher-order skills; generating and correcting student writing; individual coaching; developing individualized programs; leading Socratic discussions; eliciting active student participation; varying techniques and student groupings; providing feedback to students; humanizing knowledge (i.e., making it personally relevant); motivating students; fostering creativity.

- Internships as a key part of the training--some studies maintain that training should be wholly school based.

Inservice development: Many researchers believe that to teach well a teacher must continue to be a learner and that the school must be a learning community that offers teachers numerous and varied learning opportunities. These opportunities are costly, requiring at least replacement personnel. Recommendations in other areas (for example, the use of qualified business and community personnel for teaching and nonteaching duties) begin to suggest how the more costly of the following recommendations could be feasible.

- Regular evaluations, by master teachers, with feedback and support.

- Opportunity to observe others' classes.

- Video tape for self-improvement.

- Sabbaticals every seven years for study.

- Fellowships and summer terms for planning and development of new teaching materials and techniques.

• Workload: Many studies recommend reducing the workload and/or employing teachers for additional time with pay, so that teachers can give adequate attention to the professional duties that require their time. In Japan, whose students surpass ours in achievement tests in a number of areas, high school teachers teach only 15 hours a week. (The studies do not make clear how their pay relates to the pay of U.S. teachers.) Recommendations include:

- A teacher should teach no more than four classes and one seminar.

- A teacher should teacher no more than 80 students. (This recommendation of a small student-teacher ratio is made on behalf of both students and teachers. For teachers, it is claimed that large numbers of unfamiliar students contribute to teacher burnout.)

- Adequate time should be allowed for correcting student papers, preparing for classes.

- Teachers should have no nonteaching duties. This recommendation is made by most studies that address the conditions of teaching; a few studies, however, suggest that teacher participation in extracurricular activities is beneficial in that it helps teachers to learn about different facets of their students' abilities and interests.

- Teachers should be employed for an additional month entirely for purposes of jointly planning the local school program.

• Support in Discipline: Teachers should be supported by a clear code, fairly applied, and by administrative personnel willing to back them up.

• Increased Autonomy: Teachers should have control over classroom aspects of the improvement process and choice of materials and evaluation methods, and they should have a voice in teacher hiring. (In view of the frequent recommendation for more autonomy, it is interesting that Goodlad's survey of teacher perceptions found that teachers felt they had enough autonomy in teaching matters, but not enough in establishing conditions that affected the teaching task, e.g., classroom size.)

● Reduced Isolation: Studies recommend time for teachers to visit other classes and other schools and weekly meetings for planning and collegiality. Lipsitz describes (with the understanding of someone who has spent much time inside schools) the positive context for teachers in "successful" schools organized in small units:

> Most striking is the lack of adult isolation in these schools, unlike the experiences that so many of the teachers recount from their previous teaching assignments. Common planning and lunch periods, team meetings, and team teaching encourage constant communication and allow for high levels of companionship....The gratification of adult relationships in the schools can tide a teacher over the bad days when young adolescents go for the jugular, and can leave teachers open to enjoying the good times when they are the most enthusiastic, creative, and appreciative students one can teach. (p. 185)

● Career Ladder and Pay: At the beginning of the current period of concern about high school education, an early realization of researchers and the public was how poorly teachers' salaries compared with those of other professionals. In an effort both to improve salaries and to encourage the better teachers, recommendations for "merit pay" came from several quarters. When teacher organizations explained their opposition to the merit pay concept, more acceptable plans began to appear. Several plans have been praised as exemplary by a number of the studies. Two, the Charlotte-Mecklenberg and Tennessee plans, propose career ladders that base advancement and increased pay on quality teaching performance (systematically evaluated) and increased responsibility in training other teachers. A third plan, in the Houston Independent School District, gives incentive pay for teachers

206

who teach in inner-city schools or in areas of critical staff shortage.

The Southern Regional Education Board publications give many examples of promising plans for career ladders and pay scales being implemented by states and districts. For example, in one Texas community teachers designated as "academic coaches" receive an additional $5,000. They add to their regular responsibilities such things as teaching in summer school, extended hours, and curriculum development. Most plans included these features:

- Advancement opportunities tied to teaching performance.

- "Rungs" on the ladder that include apprenticeship, teacher, senior teacher, and master teacher levels.

- Eleven-month contracts to allow for planning, curriculum development, work with students with special needs.

- Increased salary for all teachers in all fields.

● The Shortage of Mathematics and Science Teachers: Several studies acknowledge the problems caused by the shortage of mathematics and science teachers and provide some concrete suggestions for relieving it:

- Employ as part-time teachers qualified noncertified people, e.g., retired scientists, industry personnel.

- Provide special incentives from business community-- fellowships, summer employment, dual career options, updating courses.

- Offer differentially higher salaries for teachers in these fields (not supported by most studies).

The wealth of recommended improvements for teachers, more than recommendations in any other area, prompts the reaction that the suggestions are attractive but Utopian. Where are all the resources to come from? Chapter five touches on implementation issues; here we will simply note that some of the recommendations dovetail. It can help to implement several recommendations simultaneously.

207

For example, increased use of community volunteers can relieve teachers of nonteaching duties; qualified industry personnel teaching part-time may reduce the actual teaching load.

Principals

The studies see the principal as the key figure in establishing a learning climate and the type of school organization and scheduling that will be needed to support the recommended changes in teaching methods and curriculum. All studies that deal with the issue of autonomy and decision hierarchies within school systems, state that specific educational programming and school organization decisions should be school based, thereby giving the principal the primary role in decision making. The studies generally maintain that it is, in fact, the principal's responsibility to protect the autonomy of the school. To enable principals to do this, the studies recommend extensive and varied preservice training opportunities and inservice opportunities for individualized training, collegial interaction, and renewal.

The only disagreement among the recommendations are over the role of the principal. While most studies seem to imply that the principal's role should extend from school administration to instructional leadership, some propose that a principal's role covers only part of this spectrum.

Below are some specific recommendations the studies make for principals.

● Recruitment: In contrast simply to "plucking a teacher from the classroom," several studies recommend that school districts establish a description of desired characteristics, develop a pool of candidates, and invest in training and apprenticeships.

● Training: A principal's training should be the same as that for teachers, to give background for instructional leadership and, in addition, special managerial expertise.

208

● Role: Most studies see the principal's role as instructional leader, with descriptions of this role ranging from influencing classroom practice and giving workshops on teaching to organizing the conditions for good teaching. These conditions include use of time; class size; composition of groups; curriculum coordinaton across levels; climate of high expectations; collegial staff development; protection of teachers from outside pressures; disciplinary code and support. However, Goodlad's image of the principal is as head administrator, with someone else as head teacher to provide instructional leadership. On the other hand, Sizer maintains that a principal's main role should be that of head teacher and that another executive should manage administration.

● Inservice Training: Principals need continuing education in instructional leadership, individualized with regard to particular strengths and weaknesses, and supplemented with opportunities to learn from site visits, conferences, collegial interaction.

● Higher Salary.

● More Autonomy: Principals should have control over school budgets, specific curriculum planning, and the hiring and firing of teachers.

The School Plant

All studies that mentioned the condition of school plants maintain that there are serious problems requiring more funding than most individual communities can provide. Specific recommendations include the following:

− Many schools must correct serious safety problems.

− Many schools offer bland, unattractive environments; Goodlad notes that businesses are much more conscious of the effect of the environment on employees and deliberately create an attractive environment to enhance productivity. He suggests that schools do the same.

− Many older buildings are not amenable to approaches suggested in this set of reports; either new construction

or major alterations are needed to create school buildings that allow a large school to function in small
units; convey the sense of a small, knowable community;
can be personalized by students and faculty; and can
serve the needs of different-size classes working in
lecture, discussion, and coaching modes.

- Laboratory equipment must be updated and replaced in
many schools.

- A number of studies recommend federal help to fund the
refurbishment of school plants, and Boyer recommends that
a federal School Building and Equipment Fund be established to give communities low-cost loans and other help
needed to make critically needed improvements without
delay.

Institutions and Individuals Outside the School System

Many of the studies acknowledge that the number of tasks
assigned to high schools today has gotten out of hand.
Faced with an exponential growth in the information and
skills that society wants conveyed and, at the same time,
a student population that is, for a plethora of reasons,
less interested in learning than were earlier genera-
tions, high schools cannot perform their entire task in
isolation. Many studies recommend supportive roles for
institutions and individuals outside school systems.
Because this report is written for local educators, we
will not analyze what others are asked to do, but will
simply present a list so that local educators know what
help is being offered or recommended.

● Governmental Agencies: Governmental agencies at all
levels are asked to provide schools with more funding and
more autonomy, within a framework of guiding principles
and goals for education. The federal government has been
asked to fund any programs it requires, to give special
aid to locations that are unusually deprived or have a
new and large influx of immigrant children (along the
model of impact aid to areas with a large proportion of
armed forces personnel), and to establish a School
Building and Equipment Fund to give immediate aid,
possibly in the form of low-interest loans, to schools

needing costly refurbishment. Several of the studies
have called for the development of new curricula but have
not specified how such curricula would be funded; it may
be envisioned that federal and state agencies, private
agencies, and business and industry would collaborate in
the funding.

State governments are asked to develop higher standards
for high school education; provide guidance to schools on
policies, practices, and programs that foster excellence;
require local use of state curriculum guidelines; assure
equality in state distribution of resources; and collaborate with local districts in the provision of enrichment
programs (for example, at least one state has established
a special residential academy for gifted students).

Several studies make recommendations for funding plans
that could be employed at either federal or state levels
or at both. The National Center for Policy Analysis
study (The Failure of Our Public Schools: The Causes and
a Solution) recommends that school districts be awarded
funds in correlation with achievement rather than attendance (the study presents its view on why relating funding to attendance is counterproductive). Another study
recommends the use of voucher plans, with the rationale
that such plans would result in more diversity and volunteerism, characteristics sought by many of the current
studies.

School districts are asked to establish "rational" feeder
patterns for school attendance so that each school has a
self-identified community; give more autonomy to individual schools, reserving to themselves the responsibility
of raising adequate funds and providing overall curriculum guidelines; reduce layers of bureaucratic authority
and reduce incentives for bureaucratic careers so that
more resources are channeled into teaching; identify and
train a pool of candidates for principalships; and provide consultants to help a school build its capacity for
improvement.

Individual schools are asked to be responsible for
developing specific course content, developing the school
budget, developing long-term staffing plans, and purchasing materials—all, of course, within general dis-

211

trict guidelines. It is emphasized frequently that the individual school must be the locus of decision making and the improvement process for two reasons: to engage the interest of the school staff, and because the school staff best understands the needs of the students.

● <u>Communities</u>: The community the school serves is asked to provide volunteers willing to relieve teachers of non-teaching duties to share their expertise with students.

● <u>Parents</u>: Parents are asked to support teacher morale by simply giving praise when it is due, and to establish conditions conducive to students' doing homework.

● <u>The Business Community</u>: Leaders in business, industry, and labor are being looked to as a major source of aid in bringing about the recommended improvements, and the military is also asked to help in the nonfunding aspects of the following: provide schools with knowledge of the skills that will be needed for jobs now and in the near future; establish partnerships with schools to develop training opportunities and facilities; provide scholarships and loans for prospective teachers; award teaching fellowships and provide dual career options for teachers; explore ways of employing teachers in professional roles during the summer, while extending their salaries; release employees to teach part-time in the school, especially employees with children in the schools and employees with science and math expertise; lend employees to the schools to provide management expertise; make vocational and scientific equipment available to the schools.

● <u>Colleges and Universities</u>: Colleges are asked by many studies to phase in higher entrance requirements and to make such higher requirements well known, with the anticipated result being that high school students will take more challenging programs and work harder at them. (These higher standards are not to be used to exclude minorities or disadvantaged students.) Universities are asked to establish partnerships with school systems and provide teacher development programs. Community colleges are asked to establish programs that permit students who have either dropped out of high school or been expelled to continue their education when they are ready to return.

212

● <u>Museums and Youth Organizations</u>: These organizations are asked to contribute to the teaching of science by establishing programs and rich environments for science experiences outside of school.

The Improvement Process

The studies that focus on the improvement process do so because they believe that the way a change is instituted determines how effective and long lasting the change will be. Several studies, in fact, suggest that the most important improvement a school can make is to develop a permanent capacity for change, a capacity that would allow the school continually to improve itself and to respond to the changing needs of both its students and the outside world. This capacity consists of the development of a planning group of school staff members and community and district representatives, and an agreed-upon process for articulating needs and designing and implementing changes to meet them.

The studies offer a number of different models for the improvement process, all of which include the following elements:

● The vision and determination of key people.

● Clear, shared goals for the improvement.

● Participation of those who will be responsible for carrying out the process.

● Awareness of the interconnectedness of all aspects of education, and planning that takes this interconnectedness into account.

For specific models, we refer readers to the reports in the fourth section of chapter three.

Conclusion

What stands out most from these many pages of recommendations? We believe that the following six summarizing recommendations embody the spirit of many of the changes recommended:

• A core curriculum for all that is organized, sequenced, uncluttered (fewer facts, more in-depth understanding), adaptable, and amenable to individualization.

• Emphasis on the teaching of higher-order skills.

• More individualization of teaching and more continuity in teacher-student relationships.

• More variety in teaching methods with emphasis on methods that foster active student participation.

• The teacher as the key figure in bringing about the recommended improvements, and a new "Three R's" for teachers: Room, Resources, and Respect.

• School reorganization based on small units.

The list is simple, but that by no means implies that the process of change will be easy. The outpouring of advice from the current studies is truly a case of "easier said than done." We believe that the following statement made by Harold Howe II is an insightful assessment of the situation for local school systems:

> ...local school districts and schools have been slower [than states] to move, not because they are less responsible than the states, but because they are more so. They actually see children, parents, and teachers every day, and they are acutely aware of the complexities of producing changes that are well conceived. Also, they have been through many quick fixes engendered from on high and are suspicious of these....any ultimate benefit American education will receive from its new turmoil will come more from these local responses than from those at higher levels of political decision making, but I do not mean to indicate by this statement that state and national responses are unimportant. They are just less important.

CHAPTER FIVE
From Advice to Action

There is a considerable gap between the summary of recommendations presented in this book and the information
that schools and school districts need in order to embark
on an improvement mission. This chapter attempts to
place a few lights to mark the way across a very large
void. Its goal is to help school principals and planning
groups make a start in choosing among a vast array of
possibilities for improvement.

Those who implement the changes will need to have information on such questions as, What is involved in the
improvement process? Where can the necessary resources
be obtained? What are the considerations in finding a
place to start?

This chapter is addressed to all involved in the improvement process, but primarily to principals. The studies
argue persuasively that the most important level for
change is that of the "building," or individual school,
and that the key person in planning for and carrying out
change is the principal.

What Is Involved in the Improvement Process?

General recommendations for accomplishing change include
the following:

● Planning for improvement should be a continuing
process.

● Planners should start with a long-term view based on
their vision of excellence, not with a single problem.

● There is no one vision of excellence. Each principal,
each school must develop an individual vision of excellence, based on exposure to many views.

● Basic to the improvement planning process is the
establishment of a planning group that represents all who
will be involved in making the improvements.

215

● The plan of action developed by the group should specify clear objectives for improvement activities, anticipated costs of the activities, personnel responsible for carrying out each activity, evaluators, and how and when each activity will be evaluated.

● Improvement plans should be flexible enough to change as obstacles arise.

● It is important to use accurate information as the basis for planning. The October 1983 Association for Supervision and Curriculum Development (ASCD) Curriculm Update notes, for example, that when a number of schools that were planning improvements inventoried their courses for desired learning opportunities, they were surprised to find that many of the opportunities already existed—but only for top students. The improvement needed turned out to be more one of broader access than of new curriculum development.

For more detail, rationale, and approaches to the improvement process, we refer readers to the studies in the last section of chapter three, "Studies That Focus on the Improvement Process," and to a helpful publication of the American Association of School Administrators, Planning for Tomorrow's Schools.

In addition to suggesting ground rules for the improvement process, recent studies have made some interesting observations about the process:

● A publication of the Effective Schools Movement, Creating Effective Schools, notes that change is often resisted by a school because of fear of failure, unfamiliarity with new programs, or insecurity about personal competence. ASCD suggests additional reasons why teachers may react cautiously: "With declining enrollments and tight budgets, many teachers are naturally skeptical when administrators start talking about what students 'really need to know'; it sounds like a ploy for reducing staff."

And the National Science Board's Working Group on Chemistry Education gives insights into how resistance to change can operate in one academic field:

216

Barriers preventing implementation of new chemistry-teaching ideas include (1) The inherent resistance of textbook publishers to innovation or change; (2) A difference in the level of "respectability" associated by teachers with instruction in theoretically oriented chemistry (high prestige) and applied (descriptive) chemistry (lower prestige); (3) The dynamics of the oft-cited principle that one tends to teach the way one was taught; (4) The general lack of suitable resource materials to support the infusion of more applied, real-world examples into current courses. (Educating Americans for the 21st Century, Source Materials, p. 41)

According to Creating Effective Schools, a study of schools in the change process found, ironically, that "schools with rising achievement were often characterized by staff dissension, disagreement, and dissatisfaction, while schools with declining achievement were marked by complacent and satisfied staff." The remedies that Creating Effective Schools suggest for some of these problems are that the process must be a collective one involving all the staff, and that "...the potential for conflict should be recognized in advance and put 'out on the table.' In this way it will be understood and recognized as a necessary and valuable part of the change process."

● To complete an improvement plan takes time: usually from five to seven years. Even developing a strategic plan involving 20 to 25 people can take four to six months. Administrators, staff, and others involved must have realistic expectations about what is possible in a specified time span.

● The long process of change need not be characterized only by conflict and tension. It can be rewarding in itself. Remember the "halo" effect. The attention, public good will, and resources a school may attract by improving itself can create positive outcomes which, in turn, create the momentum and self-esteem needed for the improvement to succeed.

Where Can the Needed Resources Be Found?

Views on the cost of making improvements vary. One analysis notes that simply raising teachers' salaries enough to make them competitive with other jobs would cost between $11 and $22 billion; other studies focus on efficient use of existing resources. Gary L. Phillips of the Institute for Development of Educational Activities, Inc. (I/D/E/A), illustrates the latter approach:

> Since our planning process mobilizes new participants including new roles for students, parents, and the private sector, we have been able to introduce significant changes in the school programs without additional expenditures. Or, in cases where some initial expenditure was necessary for staff development, the resulted program improvements have reduced program costs more than the amount invested in the improvement endeavor. (Insuring Continuous Improvement of Instructional Programs, p. 1)

The late Ronald R. Edmonds supported the same view in an article describing schools that are equally effective with children from high and low social classes:

> While all of these programs would advocate increased financial support for schools, their designs focus on more efficient use of existing resources. (Educational Leadership, December 1982, p. 10)

The truth about costs probably turns out to be somewhere between enormous and insignificant. For the local educator, it is plain that despite the most skillful use of resources, some types of improvements will be costly; help in paying these costs, however, may come from state, federal, or private sources.

Major improvement of school plants and laboratories and acquisition of adequate supplies have to have a cost, but many studies are optimistic that industrial or business "partners" will provide supplies or facilities or otherwise share the cost, and one study recommends that the federal government establish a fund to help with needed reconstruction.

The development of such new science and mathematics curricula as those recommended by the National Science Board
and such new guidance instruments as the Student Achievement and Advisement Test recommended by Ernest L. Boyer,
in High School, will involve costs for both the development process and the purchase of new materials. The
studies do not make clear who is to develop the new
materials and how the costs are to be financed. Teachers
and guidance personnel may develop materials for their
own schools, but time will be needed for the work. If it
is done during the school year, replacements for teachers
will have to be paid. If it is done during the summer,
teachers will need additional pay. Studies hopefully
suggest that local business "partners," local newspapers,
or other interested agencies might be willing to fund
fellowships for summer development work.

The acquisition of staff development and consulting services (on, for example, strategic planning, or updating
vocational education) will have a cost, but school systems have found approaches that both minimize costs and
produce other benefits. As illustrated in Paideia Problems and Possibilities, teacher education costs can be
kept low if the first teachers to learn a new technique
become the teachers of others. The added benefits are
collegial interaction and learning something better by
teaching it. The studies suggest that schools may be
able to obtain management and vocational counseling at
little cost, again, if they succeed in developing partnerships with local business or industry; and, if they
do, this relationship might produce some of the other
benefits discussed earlier. The studies also suggest
that colleges and universities might cooperate in
providing teacher education, but they may be no more able
than the schools are to bear the cost.

What will be the costs of the lower student-adult ratios
and new responsibilities and approaches being asked of
teachers and guidance personnel? Will supplementary
personnel be needed? Will local business and industry
contribute the services of volunteer personnel that many
studies recommend? Will these people be effective in the
roles to which they are assigned? Can students doing
peer teaching help significantly? Can students perform,
as service to the school, some of the teachers' former

nonteaching duties? Examples in the studies show that schools do seem to be able to redefine teachers' jobs without great additional personnel costs. No doubt this is because the redefining has been professional up-grading: removing nonprofessional duties and giving teachers the opportunity to learn new skills and the challenge of new teaching situations, circumstances that are in themselves rewarding. Inherent rewards notwith-standing, the studies strongly support raising teachers' salaries but do not generally take positions on where the funds should come from.

Some recommended changes do not immediately suggest sig-nificant new costs. They range from small but important ones such as finding ways other than the public address system to disseminate messages and school-wide informa-tion, and establishing a disciplinary code, to more complex ones such as reorganizing a large school into subunits.

One resource almost all the changes depend on is informa-tion on what to anticipate and how to carry out the par-ticular change. The information is almost always to be found in the experience of other schools and other educa-tors who have pioneered changes. This information may be formulated and conveyed by consultants or publications, or it may be obtained by contacting the pioneering schools. Some of the studies are rich in implementation examples, and, if they do not give full details of steps along the way, they identify schools and systems so that readers can contact them for further information. The studies that give such examples include the following:

Paideia Problems and Possibilities has an appendix that gives full descriptions of the·implementation of Paideia programs in several systems and schools. This is particularly interesting material because the change involved is large and comprehensive.

The Southern Regional Education Board (SREB) published two studies, The Need for Quality and Meeting the Need for Quality: Action in the South. The latter, written two years after the first study presented recommenda-tions, gives numerous examples of ways that states, systems, and schools have responded to the call for improvement. Topics include upgrading the teaching profession, the education of principals, the raising of college admissions requirements, and establishing special academies for gifted students. Of most interest to local planners may be examples of business-sponsored adopt-a-school programs and guidance counselors' work with local businesses that results in updating vocational guidance and education.

The National Science Board's report, <u>Educating Americans for the 21st Century</u>, gives examples of the ways that states are funding implementation of computer education programs.

The <u>University/Urban School National Task Force Conference Proceedings</u> contain papers that describe the implementation of programs designed to teach reasoning skills and to remedy learning difficulties.

The Ford Foundation's <u>City High Schools: A Recognition of Progress</u> cites examples from around the country of the ways that large, urban high schools have improved the climate for learning.

I/D/E/A's case study, <u>A Successful Building-Based Approach to School Improvement in a U.S. Urban High School</u>, gives many examples of the creative use of human resources in bringing about change.

What Are the Considerations in Finding a Starting Place?

One dictum about educational change is that since all aspects of an educational system are interconnected, anyone wishing to make a significant change must not try to do just one thing, but work with the entire system. Whether or not this dictum is correct, it is paralyzing. Harold Gores, a former superintendent of the Newton, Massachusetts, schools has a more helpful view:

> You can grab a spider's web at any point and any motion you make will shake the whole thing.

In other words, innovators do not have to plan to affect a whole system, because, in fact, they cannot avoid doing

221

it. A spider's web is an appropriate image for the tangle of processes, resources, and structures that go into the activity of providing education.

Given a vision, a planning group, and a planning process, where does one grab the spider's web? What criteria does one use to decide? Harold Howe II, former U.S. Commissioner of Education, suggests that in the matter of finding a starting point, the precedents of other schools and studies may not be the best guide. Seeing diversity as one of the great strengths of American education, he hopes that schools will start in different places and take different paths to improvement. Following is a series of questions that planning groups can consider in choosing a place to start.

● Among the recommendations that have been chosen for implementation, do some depend on other recommendations already being in place? Some recommendations are good to start with, because they set up the conditions that other recommendations need for success. For example, individualized teaching has a better chance of success in a school already organized into small units, where teachers have some continuity with students. Thus, a school might start by organizing into small units and then increase individualization in teaching practice.

While some recommendations can be addressed early, others may have to be postponed because the conditions they require for success do not exist. For example, purchasing of computers for classroom use may best be done after there has been some staff development in the use of computers so that teachers can make a knowledgeable contribution to purchasing decisions.

● Do any of the chosen recommendations reinforce each other? If so, they should be implemented simultaneously. For example, giving teachers increased time for their own education, curriculum development, and joint planning will be more feasible when, in conjunction, qualified industry personnel are brought into teaching roles to fill gaps in coverage.

● Which recommendations cost least? Introducing less intrusive ways of delivering messages and establishing a

222

relationship with local business or industry are two examples of actions for improvement that are inexpensive and have the added bonus of establishing conditions that help other actions succeed. The Education Commission of the States' Issuegram #5, "Low-Cost School Improvement," gives numerous examples of improvements that are not costly.

● For which recommendations are resources already available? Some schools may have local colleges that can help with teacher education; others have a local industry willing to help improve the school plant and facilities; and yet others have a very active parent-teacher organization that supplies volunteer personnel. Start with the recommendations that use community strengths.

● Which recommendations have the broadest effect? The Paideia program suggests that if a system cannot start with total implementation of the Paideia plan, a good "entering wedge" would be to introduce Socratic teaching at all levels. (Paideia recommends this in contrast to other partial measures of working with only certain grade levels, or coaching only some intellectual skills.) What this change would involve is arranging to have some classes no larger than 25 (which may be the case in many schools already) and probably some teacher education. Its benefits would include more variety in teaching activities, more active student participation, better teacher knowledge of students, and the introduction into the curriculum of the development of judgment. Another change with potentially broad effects, even rippling effects, is organizing a school into small units. A third change, which many claim would have an enormous ripple effect, is raising teachers' salaries.

● Which recommendations are most clearly related to the school's vision of excellence? A school or principal whose vision of excellence focuses on preparing students for skills needed in their futures may choose a starting point different from that of a school whose vision of excellence emphasizes that the school be a learning community.

* * * * *

We end this chapter where the first chapter began: with the observation that new problems arise out of attempts to solve old ones. There is no doubt that if the current improvement effort has any impact at all, it will create some problems that no one can now predict. This is acceptable so long as the "new" problems are not reversals of the gains of the recent past—the gains made in equality of educational opportunity. As long as we can preserve and build on these gains, the blend of American ingenuity, intensive effort on the part of educators and researchers, and a continuing public commitment to improvement could make the next decade a promising one for education.